THE OFF SEASON

The Newspaper Stories of Mike Lunsford

Shade Tree Press

Rosedale, Indiana

Shade Tree Press
8945 South Coxville Rd.
Rosedale, Indiana 47874
www.mikelunsford.com

Printed in the United States of America
2nd Printing, 2016

The author and publisher gratefully acknowledge the Terre Haute Tribune-Star in which the contents of this book appeared in column form from June 2005 through May 2008.

Library of Congress Control Number: 2008906774

Lunsford, Michael J. (Mike), 1956-
The Off Season: The Newspaper Stories of Mike Lunsford/Mike Lunsford
ISBN 978-0-615-23811-1 (pbk.)

For Joanie, who has always dotted my i's and crossed my t's. And to the memory of my parents.

TABLE OF CONTENTS

Chapter 2: Places

Chapter 3: Things

INTRODUCTION

by Max Jones, Editor-in-Chief of the Terre Haute Tribune-Star

---

Since mid-2005, Mike Lunsford has been treating readers of the Tribune-Star to his special brand of storytelling a couple of times a month on the front page. How his stories came to occupy such valuable newspaper real estate is a puzzle to no one but Mike.

Tribune-Star readers first became familiar with Mike's writing talents in the mid-1990s when, at the behest of then-Sports Editor Mark Bennett, he began to do a column for the sports section. The column dealt less with the intricacies of athletics and more with the people and places that make sports deeper and more interesting than statistics and final scores. Two beautifully written pieces -- one in early 2004, the other in the spring of 2005 -- found their way onto Page 1. From those instances, it was clear that Mike's stories and our front page were a perfect fit. A few months later, "The Off Season" was launched. It has been a reader favorite ever since.

Mike's special connection with his readers has a lot to do with the kinds of stories he tells -- and the way he tells them. His style features a soft, reasoned voice that often delivers wisdom borne of fundamental understanding of and sensitivity toward his chosen subjects.

As the product of parents and grandparents who loved to talk and tell stories around the dinner table and on the porch of their rural homes, Mike was destined to be a storyteller. Still, finding a "voice" and learning to capture the proper tone are not easy skills for a writer to develop.

Where did Mike's skills come from? From his love of reading and learning? From his keen sense of time and place? Perhaps. But Mike's explanation is far simpler and, as usual, laced with subtle humor. He once wrote a column in which he revealed, "I perfected my storytelling skills in the principal's office when I was in grade school, and I haven't really ever stopped."

This collection of essays demonstrates that Mike honed those skills well. With a style punctuated by salt-of-the-earth eloquence, he paints detailed word pictures as colorful as a "Salty" Seamon landscape.

Mike writes as he lives, with themes such as family, friends, home, and nature dominating his narratives. He is a country boy at heart, and his stories reflect that. He is blessed with riches bestowed upon him by awesome powers of observation.

"I think I'm a pretty wealthy man, actually, and I don't mean financially," he's said. "I think that's why my stories often deal with things of intrinsic value: old friends, yearbooks, reunions, fall days, country walks . . . that sort of thing."

No matter which of Mike's topics you find most appealing, I am confident you will find passages in this book that will move you in unpredictable ways.

So, take a seat on the porch. Relax. Prepare to laugh, to cry, to be enchanted and entertained. Best of all, prepare to feel a little closer to home.

MY THANKS

I really have no idea how it happened that I am to be called a writer and that you are reading a book with my name on the cover. My life in writing just happened ...one of those beautiful zigs in a lifetime of day-to-day zags.

Had you found me on that little patch of the planet I called home as a boy—and I almost certainly never strayed far from those few acres in central Indiana on which we lived until I had a wife and a mortgage to call my own—you would have probably discovered rocks in my pockets and the grit of creek bed sand under my nails.

But if there is anyone to thank from my childhood for turning me into a writer, it is my mother. Mom has been gone for years now, but she is never far from my thoughts. She was a reader; I am a reader and writer because of her.

Despite doing a little work for the Terre Haute Tribune-Star in college, and later as a stringer, I taught English and coached basketball and raised a family for over 15 years before I thought much about writing anything more than a grocery list. But in the fall of 1995, I got a call from Mark Bennett, the then sports editor at the Tribune-Star. "How'd you like to write a column for us?" Mark asked. I told him that I was certain I could write one story; after that I might be in trouble.

Not long after Mark became the primary feature writer at the paper—and a very good one at that—I wrote a story that really had nothing to do with sports, a habit that eventually landed my stuff on the front page. Mark and Max Jones, the paper's editor, who has graciously written the introduction to this book, gave me the chance to write "The Off Season," and the years have once again begun to roll by. For believing in me from the beginning, I thank Mark and Max and the good people at The Tribune-Star, including Assistant Editor Susan Duncan, who, although a small person, has a very big job to do, and she does it well.

There has not been a year in the past thirteen that a reader has not said to me, "You should write a book." Over that time I have received hundreds and hundreds of letters from folks who like my stories, as well as comments from hundreds more who have stopped me in a store or at a ballgame to say they've liked what I've written. A writer can't be called a writer unless he has readers, and I want to thank all of mine.

I want to also thank Jennifer Weir for her help with this project. Jennifer has taught me quite a bit about getting a book into print, especially that it takes patience. John Olsen deserves thanks too. He came to me some time ago and asked me to edit a book he had written about his life and times as a Loogootee Lion. My time as John's editor served me well, because it didn't take long for me to be inspired by his drive to see his words in print. If John hadn't gotten me busy with his book, I don't think I would have gotten busy with my own.

Thanks also need to go out to Steve Letsinger, who saw to it that I had wonderful art for the cover of this book. The watercolor painting that graces that spot is called "Senior Sycamore" and was painted by my late and good friend, D. Omer "Salty" Seamon. Steve is the curator of Rose-Hulman Institute of Technology's art collection, highlighted by its fine Salty Seamon collection of over 650 works. Thanks again, Steve.

Thanks too to my friend, Bill Wolfe. Bill is an artist and sculptor and one of the most talented men I have ever met. He designed the logo for Shade Tree Press and has been an encouraging voice in the making of this book.

I can go on thanking folks for a long time, or I can allow you the chance to start reading a few stories, but before I stop, I have to simply thank my wife, Joanie. If she had done nothing else but give me my two children, Ellen and Evan, then it would have been enough, but in everything I've done that is good for the past 30 years, she has been right beside me. To her, saying thanks is not enough.

Mike Lunsford, 2008

PREFACE

The stories in this book are primarily about the people and places and things that I have come to know by living my life in a small and quiet place, which for a man who wanted to travel the world, a rock hammer in his backpack, is an ironic spot, for there's little rock on my place, unless you count what I have brought here myself. My home is only about three miles or so from where I grew up in a sweet little community occupied solely by my family—my parents and a brother and sister, my cousins and aunt and uncle who lived across the dusty road, and my paternal grandparents, with whom we shared a driveway through the woods.

I've been told that writers really need to write about things of which they know. That bit of advice limits me considerably, and that's why hay baling or hummingbirds, windy country walks or wandering cats, family members and unfailing friends are the topics of my stories.

It was never really my intent to be a storyteller at all, but a family of eccentric folks helped change that. An example of that is a story that my cousin, Gene Lunsford, loves to tell about my dad, who passed over a dozen years ago. As you will discover in a story in the first chapter, Gene came to live with my grandparents and my dad after his father, my great uncle, Albert, was killed in World War II. Although there was more than a decade between them in age, he and Dad grew very close and there has not been a time when I've seen Gene that he does not mention my father.

As he tells it, the two of them could not get an old motorcycle they were tinkering with to start. Dad proposed that Gene attach a tow rope to the bike and pull it with a car. The cycle would not start despite the fact that Gene eventually got up to pretty impressive speeds, so fast in fact that Dad, with way too much slack in the rope, passed Gene on a descending slope.

"I'll never forget the look of shear terror on his face," Gene says with tears running down his face, "It was one of the scariest and funniest things I have ever seen."

Dad and Gene's story is typical of the kind I choose to tell. There is a unique alchemy in each of us, my family and friends and acquaintances included, that makes us individuals, that makes our stories worth hearing. I have tried to tell a few in my columns over the past years, and, ultimately, in this book.

Let me know how you like them.

Additional copies of this book are available through Mike Lunsford's website at www.mikelunsford.com

It's what you learn after you know it all that counts the most." **John Wooden**

"God grant that I may live upon this earth
And face the tasks which every morning brings
And never lose the glory and the worth
Of humble service and the simple things."

Edgar Guest

"More of us need to know our local ground, walk over it, care for it, fight for it, bear it steadily in mind."

Scott Russell Sanders

"We cannot comprehend what comprehends us."

Wendell Berry

CHAPTER ONE

PEOPLE

Stories help keep Dad alive, not only on Father's Day June 19, 2005

The last time I saw my dad alive he had just finished running his hand across the top of my head as we said our weekly goodbyes. He walked down the hallway toward the bedroom for an afternoon nap and told me he would see me later. He had just come home from the hospital and he was tired; that was nine years ago, nine years since I spent a Sunday afternoon at my parents' place watching him unwrap a fishing pole or a pocketknife and sleeping in his chair.

When I was a kid, Father's Day was always a quiet affair at our house, and it really hasn't changed over the years since I became a father myself. My dad worked away from home through the week, and Sundays after church were usually reserved for after-dinner snoozes, reading the "funny papers," and walking up the road to see what my grandparents were up to, which was usually about the same thing.

I can't say that I had many long conversations over the years with my dad; he wasn't much of a talker, and he really wasn't home that often. Even after I married and had kids of my own, he still spent only a day or two of each week at home. He was a construction worker, a jack-of-all-trades who contracted small jobs but worked long hours. He understood that as his arthritis and bad heart grew worse that he'd have to start working with his head more and his hands less, but as it turned out, it was his heart that gave out first.

Before "Arthur" got his elbows and ankles, my dad was the strongest man I ever knew. He was just under 6 feet tall, and although he barely weighed 140 pounds just out of high school, I remember him most at 220 with a bit of a belly, a crew cut, and freckles that started at the bridge of his nose and ran down each arm to a big pair of paws that often shook a bit under the strain of astronomical blood pressure.

I once saw my dad bear hug a refrigerator and walk out the door of my aunt's house with it, and when I stop to think of it, that feat of strength was typical of him, not because he used it to show off, but that he used it to help someone. He told jokes and made goofy faces for kids and bent elbows at the bar with the men who worked beside him smoothing concrete under the hot summer sun. He liked Ford trucks, the National Geographic, and old Willy's Jeeps. He was generous to a fault, and many times, much to the chagrin of my mom, brushed away the fact that many of his "friends" had taken money from him with no intention of ever paying it back.

Despite the fact that it was my mom who took on most of our religious education and made sure that the three of us kids were in church, I believe my dad understood the daily life of the Christian walk more than most people I've known. It was not unusual for my family to be joined at the supper table by some skinny waif Dad brought home from a remodeling project or job site, and often those kids would leave our house with a full stomach, clean clothes from my dresser drawer, washed hair, and a tooth brush.

My dad could not stand to see people suffer or to be in need of help, and I'd be willing to bet that there are still a good number of folks out around the County Line Road who could thank him for a changed tire, a gallon of gas, a lift into town, or an extra $10 in their pocket.

At my dad's funeral, I met several of the men who came to know him from his later days; they, too, were "rough old birds" who had lived tough lives of pounding nails, pulling wire, and backfilling ditches, but I could see that they cared for my father as if he were an older brother. By then, Dad was stooped a bit, had grown a shaggy red-gray beard, had to wear "specs" to read, and had not bothered to tell his wife and kids that he'd already had a couple of heart attacks while he was on the job. When his ankles swelled, he found it easier to walk with a cane. His front shirt pocket was always stuffed with papers and pens, and his arms and face were beet red from his days in the sun.

At the service, the minister read a passage from a story I had written about my dad for the Indianapolis Star not long before he died. It was about the time that the two of us had loaded up a trailer of trash to take to the dump. As we bounced along the hot asphalt in one of his old banged-up Jeeps, the trailer came loose, did a couple of pirouettes, and spewed junk from ditch to ditch before coming to an inglorious halt in the middle of the road. We stooped in the heat and the itch of Queen Anne's Lace and ironweeds along the road for a good while and picked up the trash as best we could.

Dad mumbled under his breath for a few minutes as he hitched up the trailer again, but then he began to laugh. He laughed as the sweat poured out of him, and it seemed to me that his freckles grew as large as nickels as we worked together in the broiling heat.

It is not only on Father's Day that I remember my dad, Dan, and whenever I meet someone who knew him, they always have a story to tell me. In a way, those stories keep him alive for my family and me.

As a kid, I used to think my dad was a pretty big man. I still do.

Educators teach some things that can't be measured by any test August 6, 2005

My sophomore English teacher in high school was Dorothy Grant. She was thin and gray-haired, and prim, and exact, and kind. She was demanding too; she thought that her students needed to be challenged, and we were. I'm thankful to have had her as my teacher, even though she left my papers bleeding red and often implored me to both speak up in class and sit up straight in my seat.

Mrs. Grant was cut from a bolt of pretty stern cloth. She was immaculate in dress, exact in speech, well-read, and intense. She scared most of my classmates to death, and when she announced that we would be starting the year off with the reading and discussion of William Shakespeare's "Henry IV," we collectively wilted.

What I recall most from that experience is that I enjoyed reading the lines that Shakespeare placed in the mouth of his braggart rogue, Falstaff, and that the Bard was a pretty perceptive guy when it came to understanding how people worked and thought and acted.

Mrs. Grant demanded that we discuss the play in class every day. She taught us about anachronisms and irony, archaic words, and Shakespeare's life. It's been more than 30 years since I sat in her windowless room and wondered why she liked to wear a neck scarf every day, how she could know so much, and just why we were reading that play to begin with. A lot has changed in education since that time, supposedly for the better.

Mrs. Grant evidently believed that every student she had in English 10 could understand Shakespeare, could understand anything if he or she worked at it. I think she realized that "Henry IV" wasn't going to land any of us more attractive career opportunities or help us pull down the big bucks. Reading it wouldn't qualify us for a special diploma or academic honors, and it wasn't going to make our resumes sparkle.

I think Mrs. Grant wanted us to read the play to make us more civilized; I think she wanted a roomful of restless kids to become more cultured; I think it was to teach us a little history, to help us better appreciate our language, to be better readers and more expressive writers, and, ultimately, to teach us that being educated is an entirely different thing than simply getting a diploma.

When we'd whine and ask why we were studying this or reading that, I remember that she'd quote Robert Browning: "A man's reach should exceed his grasp," she'd say. I'm not sure I understood that then, but I do now.

To my knowledge, Mrs. Grant never used the word "standard," never spoke about remediation. She didn't bug us to study our test-taking strategies as a way to score our way to success when we encountered the state tests; there were no state testing programs—no ISTEP, no Core 40 exams—then. She just wanted us to read the play, remember some of it, and enjoy it. Some of my classmates hated it; most of us liked it despite our griping.

I read a Newsweek magazine column by Anna Quindlen with interest a few weeks ago. In it, she lamented the fact that there is a worrisome trend in schools: "Our education system is broken; accountability and standards will fix it. This is the mantra of government testing programs, from local certifications to the federal No Child Left Behind program, which might as well be called No Child Left Untested."

Quindlen went on to say: "And what does this metastasizing testing, for every subject, at every level, at every time of the year, do to kids? It has to mean that students absorb the message that learning is a joyless succession of hoops through which they have to jump, rather than a way of understanding and mastering the world. Every question has one right answer; the measure of a person is a number. Being insightful, or creative, or heaven forbid, counterintuitive counts for nothing."

I couldn't agree more. One of my biggest fears with standardized testing, and the competition that schools are being forced into as they vie for shrinking state monies, is that many of our students are equating passing the tests with being educated. Some are already convinced of this, and yet many others are equally certain that failing the tests proves that they are incapable of being educated at all. I had a student last year who fell through the cracks. He was pretty bright, hated to admit that he was actually enjoying some of the work we were tackling in class, and seemed to be growing more confident every week for me But, he hadn't managed to pass the ISTEP with three dry runs under his belt; he dropped out of school this spring.

I recently administered a Core 40 test to my English 11 students: three 45-minute sessions composed of multiple choice questions, short-answer writing questions, and an essay. It's the newest exam on the horizon in Indiana high schools, an exit test for core classes designed to check if the teachers are teaching and the students are learning. To be sure, I feel students completing their junior year should be able to pass the test: most of my students did. But what the test tested bothered me.

Although Indiana's adopted state English standards for juniors call for a rather heavy dose of quality American literature, the test itself really covers a few "power standards," chosen, of course, by the makers of the tests. There was no mention of Mark Twain on this year's test, no passage by Ernest Hemingway or John Steinbeck; there was no Poe, no Thoreau, no Ernie Pyle.

What are we giving up by teaching to these tests? Are we educating kids, or are we processing them? I have doubts that No Child Left Behind and ISTEP are actually preparing them for the workplace, for parenting, for college or trade school. I have no doubt whatsoever that we are trading away bits and pieces of what may seem to be worthless or unimportant to many, but in the long run helps us be better, more humane and well-rounded people.

If Dorothy Grant were still teaching today, I think she'd still expect her students to memorize facts, diagram sentences, speak up in class, and pay attention. She wouldn't gear her teaching toward a yearly standardized test, wouldn't spend much of her class time showing students how to be better-educated guessers on multiple choice questions, either.

Over the years, I had many good teachers. Like Mrs. Grant, they pretty well taught what they wanted to teach, how they wanted to teach it. They picked and chose what they were going to teach, sometimes just because it held a good life lesson, or was traditional, or was simply hard work.

When I remember my best teachers and what they taught me, it seems as though I recall a kaleidoscope of their qualities: Mrs. Byers was Phyllis-Diller funny; Mrs. Moore always taught with a smile on her face; Mr. Miller was drill-sergeant strict but desperately wanted us to learn; Mr. Wunker was encouraging and silently tended to his plants; Miss Soyak was quiet and loved Dickens; Mrs. Vaught made me love music even though the only instrument I mastered was the radio; Mr. Bodie wanted us to look to the stars.

I could make a longer list of those wonderful people, too long to go over here, but all of those teachers, and many more in my life, were unique, not homogenized cardboard cutouts who taught toward a test, and I thank them for teaching me things that no test can measure.

Repainting a portrait of an artist in fall October 3, 2005

It is in the fall that I think of Salty Seamon the most. All it seems to take is a trace of orange in a sugar maple's leaves, or a scent of leaf smoke in the early evening air to remind me of him, of his passion for painting, of his natural curiosity, of his need to see and create beautiful things.

When he died some years ago at 86, I wrote a story for the Tribune-Star called "The Salty I Knew." What the title should have read perhaps was "The Salty I Will Always Know," because even now, when I see one of his watercolors, I feel a familiarity to the place he's captured, to the memories I have of him as he hunkered down over his framing table or swirled a well-worn brush in a chipped coffee cup of gray water.

I think Salty was one of the luckiest men I've ever known. His talent was real, not just good fortune; he worked hard at his craft. He was lucky because he had always known exactly what he wanted to do with his life, had known, in fact, that he wanted to be an artist since before he went to grade school down in Gibson County.

"I was born, laid around all that day, and have been painting ever since," he used to say. He once told me that he still had the first paintbrush he'd ever used; I had no reason to doubt him.

I knew of Salty before I ever knew him. He lived just a soybean field away from my home place when I was a kid, and all I really knew about him, despite the fact that my brother, John, used to drive back Salty's lane to visit him for an impromptu painting lesson in his self-built studio, was that he was thin and had a white mustache and that there was always a scent of pine and crabapple about his place.

It was not until Salty was an old man—really his last 10 years—that I came to know him. For years I had traipsed across his property to hunt mushrooms, knocked at his door to ask for Halloween treats, or had negotiated his pine-lined drive with my brother to deliver groceries in the worst of snowy weather. My only regret in knowing Salty was that I never really took the time to know him longer.

He was generous, opinionated, industrious, inventive. I used to stop by in the early evenings after he was back in his studio from a quick supper. Salty was almost always away from his brushes and paints by that time of the day, standing at a table he used to finish his framing. He put in as much or more time in cutting and creating the frames for his work than he had in painting them. He even cut his own glass, and often took one of his own homemade hand tools to poke faux worm holes in a frame's wood to make it appear older than it was. I've often wondered if the folks who cleaned out Salty's studio after his death really knew what purpose that assortment of rollers and nails and gadgets lying on that table really did for him.

He'd sit in a denim shirt and red suspenders with his legs crossed, his left arm held at the wrist by his right hand, always ready it seemed to me for some news, some discovery, some word of the day. We'd sit for an hour or so as the sunlight crept ever lower through the redbuds to the west of his studio's big windowpanes, gabbing about the government, about the state of things, about our families. He hated being sick, not because he felt sorry for himself, but because he couldn't keep as busy as he once did. Activity was everything to him, strange it seemed because his work often reflected man's need for peace and quiet and rest:

that life should sometimes be as lazy as leaves piling themselves up along some lonely country road.

Of all of Salty's paintings, there are two that I keep in the presence of my memories. The first is of a huge sycamore that stood near the railroad tracks at Atherton, in northern Vigo County. "Senior Sycamore" still reminds me of how graceful Salty's trees were, how they seemed to reach their branches out like arms toward the sky, how authentic they seemed in his wash of colors.

The second, a snowscape, is called "Winter's Blanket." In it, the tops of late fall grasses stick their heads up through a heavy layer of white; an old gate leans at one end as it leads the viewer's eye to the ridgeline bordering a field that fades into a horizon of atmospheric blue and gray. I know that place; I played there as a boy, and only in my thoughts will I probably ever go there again—except through Salty's steady hand and delicate brush.

A new-found friend of mine, Sister Margaret Quinlan, likes to read about the value of what we have and make of home, of a specific place. She recently sent a line to me from May Sarton's journal, "At Seventy." In it, Sarton wrote, "Adventures may be for the adventurous, but home is where the real things are sown and reaped, where in the end, the real things happen."

Salty may have been a lifetime older than I was; Sarton may be someone with whom I have little in common. But I think I know how they felt about their places in the world, the spots where they felt as comfortable as an old shoe or a favorite pair of jeans. I am a lucky man to have known an artist who enriched me, not because he gave me a bargain on a print, a bit of advice, or even his precious time.

If we take the time to stop and look at Salty's work, we may also see that a leaning barn or birds on a wire or even a layer of snow balanced on a split-rail fence can be some of the best real things in life.

If you see me, just wave
December 12, 2005

I come from a long line of wavers; you know, people who wave to other people whether it be from a yard or driving down the road or walking into the supermarket. I think waving makes us a little more civilized, a bit more worthy of being called human.

My Grandpa Roy was a waver from way back, and since I spent so much time tagging along with him, I guess I acquired the habit. He'd make a point of waving to total strangers—not just people he knew—as he walked into Morgan's Variety Store or mowed the church lawn. We used to make an annual journey to Tennessee when I was a boy, and I noticed that he waved to folks all the time. I used to think that he almost over-waved; he had to have had a very stout wrist.

Along with watching the stars as they make their appearance or the sun as it slips below the horizon, I've managed to gather almost enough material while on my evening walks to write a doctoral thesis on waving. Of course, none of this is supported by hard science; I'm a bit like Peter Warne in Frank Capra's "It Happened One Night." Warne became an expert on dunking donuts, piggybacking, and hitchhiking, just by paying attention to people.

One of the most obvious things I've learned is that a rather large number of people simply don't pay attention to my wave; they just cruise by, apparently with fixing supper or watching the big game or putting up their feet on their minds, or they're simply among that shrinking class of us on the roads who actually concentrate on keeping their cars between the ditches.

I've noticed that some drivers can't free up a hand to return a wave. That's because they have one on the wheel and the other wrapped around a cell phone. I can just hear them say, "I just passed some kook walking along the road in the cold waving to people."

Some folks acknowledge my wave, but I can tell that they're not happy about it. They wave back, but they'd clearly rather not bother with it. I'm sure that many of them really do have something serious on their minds—a sick parent or an overdue light bill—but I think some people work so hard at their jobs being busy or bossy that they feel they're letting their guard down a little to wave to me. Of course, they may know who I am and just aren't that fond of me.

The variety of waves I see fascinates me. (I've been told it doesn't take much to do that.) I usually wave by extending my right hand and giving it one single wag with the forefinger slightly extended. My cousin, Renee, has often mentioned that I wave like my grandpa did. In return, I've gotten the old head nod: once up, once down. Others give me a full hand that shakes from side to side so that I can see light between all of their digits. A lot of people just lift a single finger off their steering wheels like they're pointing to the sky, and one guy actually gave me a vigorous thumbs up as if I were in the last leg of a marathon race or preparing to break the sound barrier. I'll take it; when I drive I often see people waving with one digit, and it's clearly not a thumb.

Some wavers are a pretty enthusiastic lot. In warmer weather I've had them extend their arms out the window to wave, and I've had more than one person intentionally roll his window down just to be certain his wave was seen. If they have dark-tinted windows, I really appreciate that because otherwise I can't tell whether they're waving to me or not.

I spend considerable time in my yard clipping and snipping and mowing and raking. The portion of my lawn that runs along the road puts me in contact with a ton of potential wavers. I've almost gotten waver's elbow during the Covered Bridge Festival. My house is on a bridge route, so for two weeks I avoid any two-fisted activity like raking just so I can easily free up my waving hand. I really get a workout when motorcycle rallies or bicycle tours roll past the house. When those happen, I'm forced to become a head nodder.

I have to admit that it steams me a little when I bother to wave to someone, and they can't manage even a feeble wave in return. My wife often has to listen to me as I complain about an unacknowledged wave. I guess I feel like a door has been slammed in my face. If someone bothers to wave, you can at least wave back.

In a little experiment I recently conducted, I asked a few of my students to wave to people and then take notice as to how many waves they received for their efforts. The numbers were not encouraging. Over the course of just a day, several of my kids waved to a total of 181 people; they received 33 return waves.

My family takes a vacation every year, and no matter where we've gone, I've always been convinced that the Midwest had by far the highest percentage of friendly wavers. Maybe I've been wrong. In a particularly memorable episode of "Seinfeld," Kramer convinces nearly everyone in his apartment building that hugging one another and putting up pictures in the lobby will encourage trust and friendship in an otherwise impersonal city of millions.

I don't need a hug or a kiss; a wave is good enough. But if you do it, please, use all of your fingers.

We may all have to be Cinderella Men
March 13, 2006

A few cold months ago I went for my customary evening walk. As I squinted my way west into a setting sun, I passed a couple with their bundled and booted little boy pecking through a recently-picked cornfield looking for the ears that had been missed by the combine during harvest time.

The couple isn't destitute; their little boy isn't hungry. They're just frugal and have a few head of livestock to feed, and, I imagine, just didn't like seeing the corn go to the crows or the frequent nighttime raiding parties of deer. The boy was having fun.

Years ago I, too, walked in muddy cornfields with my grandfather, a burlap bag in my gloved hands, stooped at the waist looking for the stalks that had simply been pushed over, not cut by the corn pickers. Combines in those days weren't as efficient as they are now, and we often went home with bushels of full yellow ears for his goats and my pony. It didn't take long to learn that you simply stepped on the husks to check if they were holding treasure. And, after a while it was just that, a treasure hunt.

What may sound like child abuse or long hours of work to many today, wasn't. My gleaning days were good times, and I think they probably were for that young couple too. We weren't out there in hunger-driven desperation to feed ourselves; my grandpa just believed that it was almost sinful to waste that corn. After all, he was man who had a family to feed during the Great Depression, and as an old man he still remembered the bleak times of that age.

I remember that he hunted ginseng, trapped muskrats, and shot raccoons to make his Christmas present-buying money, and I know that if he were alive today, and if another depression hit this country, my grandpa would be one of those guys who would survive it on his own. He was tough, forged by tough times.

The whole gleaning scene may have been the subject of a Millet painting, but to me it seemed more like it came from "Cinderella Man," the Ron Howard film that tells the story of Depression-era boxer Jim Braddock. I watched the movie with my wife last fall, and as a history teacher I couldn't help but feel it gave a pretty accurate picture of the dark 1930s, despite it being less than absolutely accurate about Braddock's life. I read Michael DeLisa's biography of Braddock to fill in the movie's gray areas.

I discovered that Braddock had used his savings to buy into a taxicab business, knowing that he couldn't box forever. When the depression hit, he lost his entire $30,000 investment. Despite owning a speakeasy in New Jersey, Braddock's financial life went down the drain. A hand injury and his wife's third pregnancy eventually forced him out of the ring and onto the Weehawkenn docks.

Braddock recalled his days in the brutal winter of 1933-1934: "I worked on the docks whenever there was any work to be had. On occasions I sweated through two straight eight-hour shifts of the hardest kind of labor. . . Soon I was in debt to everybody." By the fall of 1934, Braddock became one of over 600,000 people in New Jersey to receive relief. His children were given milk; the family got $6.40 a week.

I tell this story not because the film got the next part wrong, but because it got it right. Braddock did slug himself off relief and into a championship bout with Max Baer. Prior to that fight, he said, "I'll either step from the ring champion or be carried out of it feet first."

When it was reported to the press that he had been on relief, Braddock said, "I'm not ashamed of it...I didn't mind for myself, but I couldn't let my kids starve." Braddock did ask, however, that it also be reported that after his championship qualifying fight with Art Lasky, he had given the relief fund $300; that was $60 more than his family had received from it.

I used to ask my dad and my grandpa about the Great Depression. For instance, I know my dad only wore shoes during the school year, that the upstairs bedroom where he slept was unheated, and that the wash basin was often frozen over when he got up in the morning. An orange, a little hard candy, and a pair of socks meant a good Christmas.

I know that my grandfather worked hard his whole life at a variety of jobs, including dipping enameled pans in a factory and digging ditches for the WPA. In many ways, the Depression never left either man, and in the backs of their minds, I think both thought those rough times were coming again.

By March of 1929, newly inaugurated Herbert Hoover said, "The poorhouse is vanishing among us." Little did he know that in less than six months Americans would begin their journey through a 10-year depression that would end only as World War II began. It was a time that economist John Maynard Keynes compared to the Dark Ages, while historian William Manchester called 1932 "the cruelest year." In that year, lumbermen were working for ten cents an hour, little girls invented a game called "Eviction," and a good number of people in this country were surviving on dandelions, wild onions, and violet tops.

It may sound a bit trite in an age of pessimism and bad news, but I think there are still quite a few Cinderella Men to be found. Storm clouds may be on the horizon, and it may frighten us to open our newspapers these days, but the same spirit that drove Jim Braddock to fight to feed his family, that inspired my dad and his dad to drive nails and build fences and sweat in the sun, is still around.

Gleaned fields and worn-out work boots, grimy collars and calloused hands may seem archaic to a lot of Americans in this era of computer technology and convenience shopping, and that's too bad. Hard work, and the simple values it teaches, will never be out of date.

Best wishes to an old friend moving on in life May 22, 2006

A friend of mine is about to retire from teaching after breathing the chalk dust of the classroom, the sawdust of the woodshop, and the stale sweat of the gym floor for most of the last 26 years. His career hasn't been so long by some standards – I taught with a man who put in 46 – but it's been long enough for him to know that he doesn't want to miss out on watching his grandsons grow any taller or lose any more time fooling around amidst the wonderful clutter of his own tools and freshly-cut hardwood.

I can't remember when I first met Joe Huxford—at the little country church we both attend, I suppose—but I'm a better man for knowing him and working beside him. We've spent a good many hours together teaching and coaching kids at school, but also pondering over clunky lawnmowers, hammering on summer projects, and stacking bales on hay wagons slick with the chafe of alfalfa.

Along with another teaching buddy—a crotchety veteran of 38 years who will hang up his calculators and protractors a year from now – we formed a team not unlike Larry, Curly, and Moe. All three of us have enjoyed teaching, and have respected it too.

I'm sad for me and for our kids that Joe is retiring, although I know it has to happen to us all. My kids – and I mean my own two, and the countless others who have crossed our paths over the years—couldn't have had a better example to live by or a better man to look up to than he has been. I can't tell you how many hours we "three amigos" have sat and talked about this boy or that girl, about how we hoped they could turn their lives around or wished they'd had a better life at home or a parent who cared for them. I know they were the kinds of kids that Joe thought about at night when sleep wouldn't come to him and the ceiling looked far away.

Fortunately, the abundance of the teachers I know truly care about and love children. Joe is one of those teachers. I've seen him slip kids a few dollars for meals, known him to drive others home from practices, seen him take even more under his wing to teach them how to miter a corner, shoot a jump shot, or work out an equation on the board.

Joe graduated from Rosedale High School in 1966, got his degrees from Indiana State, and first started teaching in Vermillion County, at Ernie Pyle Elementary, I think. He coached basketball and track and taught math and health and physical education, even a few subjects in which he wasn't licensed back in the days when that didn't seem to matter as much. He did get out of teaching to farm for a while, but came back to the classroom years ago because he felt that he had something to give kids. And, like all teachers, he's had a few bumps in the road to get around. Teaching may sound easy, but it's not; anyone who has ever tried it knows that to be true.

Joe is a different kind of teacher; we are cut from vastly different bolts of cloth. Where I am all straight rows and exact directions, he has always believed that somehow creation comes from chaos. He is unfazed by noise and movement and change. His wife, Linda, is constantly reminding him that at 58 he can't do everything the kids do anymore. Yet, I think this year he still gave the high jump and bench press a try. I don't know too many of our kids who would want to try to take him on in a game of "HORSE."

Just like so many of those kids, I know that when I think of Joe, I think of his kindness, of his neighborliness. It was Joe who replaced the starter on my truck as it sat in my driveway, a job that required the patience of Job and the skill of a contortionist. It was Joe who helped me cut up and drag away the limbs of an oak felled by the same windstorm that had damaged his own home. It was Joe who made the woodwork for my family room. It was Joe who was the first to step into my classroom to say he was sorry when I found out at school that my dad had suddenly passed away.

I didn't want to write this story ten years from now, or twenty. I want Joe to know now that he's meant more to our kids and our school than he believes. I suspect that for some reason he feels that he's leaving teaching without accomplishing much of what he thought he would when he started all those years ago.

That's not true. You were a success, Joe, a real success.

An evening on the town with Public Enemy Number-One June 26, 2006

Besides the macaroni salad and grilled burgers, one of the things I like best about my wife's family reunion in Indianapolis is the chance to talk to Joe DeLapp, my wife's cousin through marriage who always has a story to tell.

Last summer, as we sat at a patio table and finished off a little of my wife's cheesecake, he dropped a tale in my lap that I just couldn't resist retelling. Joe's grandparents, Albert and Dorothy DeLapp, were robbed at gunpoint by Baby Face Nelson.

I know, I know, everybody's grandparents once saw John Dillinger rob a local bank, knew who kidnapped Lindbergh's baby, or saw Al Capone stopped for a train in Terre Haute, but Joe has taken his story much further than most family folklorists. His research is convincing; Albert and Dorothy really did meet Lester Gillis, also known as Baby Face Nelson, and his .45 caliber pistol, on November 22, 1934.

Joe, a 53-year-old Atlanta, Georgia, businessman, has always had a keen interest in history and hopes that someday he'll get an article published about his grandparents' encounter with the famous killer. He first heard the story in 1965 when he was 13 years old.

"After hearing my grandfather (known to the family as Fafa or De) retell the story, and then shown newspaper clippings about it, I began to believe that it was true," says DeLapp, who has even made a Freedom of Information request for FBI documents about the case.

There were five newspapers in Chicago in 1934; at least three carried stories about the hold-up, including one clipping from the Chicago Tribune that he mailed to me. What may be the most interesting aspect of the case is that the police, and subsequently Joe, came to the same conclusion: Nelson and his two accomplices—one probably being tall, handsome John Paul Chase, who dumped Nelson's bullet-riddled body after their famous Highway 14 shootout with the FBI just five days later—were looking to kidnap Col. John J. McCormick, the publisher of the Chicago Tribune, but cornered the DeLapps and friend Walter Tower by mistake.

Albert, a successful insurance broker, and Dorothy lived in Evanston, a suburb of Chicago. On the unusually balmy night of the 22nd, the 43-year-old DeLapp and his wife left their five children with a maid and picked up Tower (the managing director of the Chicago Association of Life Underwriters) in the Rogers Park section of the city. Tower's wife had recently died, and the DeLapps wanted to treat him to the theater and dinner and drinks at a restaurant near the Loop.

During the meal, Dorothy told her husband that she felt that two men and a woman at a table nearby were eavesdropping on their conversation. Dorothy again noticed that the trio who had taken an interest in them at dinner was following them out to the parking lot. According to a story in the Chicago Daily News the next day, DeLapp eventually realized that a car was trailing his Packard, but paid little attention to it until they reached Tower's home.

As the DeLapps and Tower pulled to the curb, one of the men approached Al as he sat at the wheel and demanded to know who he was. The 6-foot, 4-inch Tower got out of the car, telling DeLapp that he'd "handle" the situation, but Tower soon had his hands in the air as he faced the stranger's shotgun. A shorter man—under 5-foot, 5-inches—with light hair, a thin mustache, and a young-looking face, slid into the front seat next to DeLapp. When DeLapp suggested that the man's handgun was a "toy," Baby Face Nelson shoved it into his ribs to suggest it wasn't. The woman, probably Nelson's wife, Helen, stayed in the other car.

Both men repeatedly asked DeLapp what his name was, and the younger man eventually grew frustrated and referred to DeLapp as "DeLoop." The Daily Times reported: "One of the men removed Tower's hat, looked him over carefully, and exclaimed, 'This ain't McCormick. We thought you were good for at least $50,000. This is a bum steer."

According to the Tribune's account, one of the perps told the DeLapps and Tower, just before robbing them, "Well, we were looking for another man who drives a car something like yours." Two factors may have led to Nelson's mistake: McCormick, like Tower, was a tall man, and Dorothy rode with Tower in the backseat, making it appear as though De was a chauffeur.

Within a few minutes, the assailants had taken $16 from Tower, $12 from Al, and $22 from Dorothy, along with her purse. Leaning over from the front seat, the 25-year-old Nelson, who was known for his explosive temper, also said, "Give me that ring." Dorothy tried to oblige but couldn't get the $1,000 engagement ring off her finger. Nelson then suggested that he was either going to club her on the head or cut her finger off if she didn't hand over the ring. The other bandit walked to the back of the car and gently helped her remove it.

The DeLapps and Tower sat in their car for 15 minutes after the robbery, just as Nelson and his pal suggested they should. They then drove to the police station to report the crime. By the following mid-day, Dorothy had been shown pictures of suspects by an FBI agent who confirmed that she was face-to-face with Nelson, a man J. Edgar Hoover simply called "the rat." Nelson had been elevated to Public Enemy No. 1 status after Dillinger's death at the Biograph Theater a few months before.

Five days later, Nelson himself was dead after killing two FBI agents in a final blaze of glory. Interestingly, writer Bryan Burroughs, in his fascinating book, "Public Enemies" (2004), describes a night in 1930 when Nelson mugged the wife of Chicago's mayor, William "Big Bill" Thompson. Nelson shoved the woman into a hotel lobby and took off with over $18,000 worth of jewelry. Her description: "He had a baby face. He was hardly more than a boy."

An odd postscript to the robbery also interests Joe DeLapp. No later than on the day after Nelson's gun battle with the Feds, a man with a purse in his hand approached Al and Dorothy's home. Speaking to 8-year-old Mitzie DeLapp, a "good-looking man," perhaps Chase, asked if the "DeLoops" were home; they weren't. Was he looking to return the purse? Was he hoping to steal the DeLapps' car had they been home? Years later, Chase admitted that he roamed Chicago suburbs in the shot-up car he and the dying Nelson used to escape the FBI.

Burroughs also wrote in his book, "When one looks back across the chasm of 70 years, through a prism of pulp fiction and bad gangster movies, there is a tendency to view the events of 1933-1934 as mythic, as folkloric...After decades in the washing machine of popular culture, their stories [Pretty Boy Floyd, Bonnie and Clyde, et al.] have been bled of all reality, to an extent that few Americans today know who these people actually were..."

Al and Dorothy DeLapp knew Baby Face Nelson was real; their grandson isn't going to forget him either.

The difference between flying the coop and leaving the nest
August 7, 2006

As you're reading this story with your morning coffee, my wife and son and I will be in the process of moving my daughter's things out of her bedroom and into her new apartment. For the most part, she's all grown up now, and she's leaving our home to make one of her own. We're all having mixed feelings about the move, and that includes the young woman who's being moved.

Our house, and that room, is the only home my daughter has ever known. My wife and I moved our meager possessions into our place only two weeks before Ellen was born. As a matter of fact, we spent our first night here sleeping on a mattress on the floor because it was too late, and we were too weary, to put our antique maple bed together. I remember telling my wife on the very day Ellen was born—the oppressively muggy August day on which I had hauled in our last loads of furniture and dishes, and helped the previous owner move their last few things out, "Whatever you do, don't have that kid tonight." Of course, Ellen made her appearance anyway.

Ever since, Ellen's room has been a nursery for her crib, a sanctuary in lonely times, a prison cell for the occasional punishment, a dormitory for sleepovers and pajama parties, and a warehouse for an incredible stash of personal memorabilia, a collection so vast that the floor joists under it will undoubtedly celebrate when its considerable weight is off their backs. But I suspect that the room's four walls will miss her a great deal too.

We don't think much about the importance of our homes until we've been gone from them awhile. Long vacations or hospital stays, college semesters or cross-country moves often leave us yearning for our childhood homes, the places that made us who and what we are. I didn't really miss the house I grew up in until my parents sold it to move up the road. Until then I had always been able to go back to the house and catch the feel and scent of home. I suppose I now know what Thomas Wolfe meant when he said, "You can't go home again," but I hope that despite that lesson my daughter and son, and their families, will always know that our house will be home to them.

In a way, Ellen's leaving reminds me of the parable of the prodigal son as described in Luke 15. Of course, the young man in the story took his inheritance and, as the Scripture says, spent it on riotous living. My kid seems to be pretty level headed, so I doubt that her new neighbors are going to be complaining much about the noise she's making or worrying about her being a threat to public safety. Unlike the boy, she'll not soon run through her money and be dining with the hogs, either. At the same time, I can foresee a smorgasbord of my wife's home-cooked care packages being foremost in Ellen's refrigerator for a while.

Her leaving kindles in me, and in my wife, a similar feeling that the scriptural boy's father must have had, too, the bittersweet hope that we've prepared our children to survive and prosper in the world independent of us, yet still in need of us all the same. We can't watch for Ellen from afar as she walks toward our house, then call for the fatted calf to be prepared, but we won't mind seeing her little blue car pull into our driveway, either. She's already made it quite clear that her two cats will have to have a little time away from living in the big city anyway.

There's a difference between flying the coop and leaving the nest. I've known parents who couldn't wait for the day when their children moved out, often to marry too early or to go broke in an attempt to have what they wanted too quickly. We've told our kids that they are welcome to live with us as long as they choose, but just as long as they understand that they live under our roof; we've made the rules in something that only slightly resembles a democracy.

Some folks may feel that our approach to child-rearing is an attitude that coddles our kids, makes them dependent on us, keeps them from dreaming big and going far. We don't think so. We believe our children are going to make it out there, not because they were babied or pampered, but because we've tried to do our best as parents whether they liked it at the time or not. Being a pair of English teachers, we also ultimately hope that our kids believe as we do in what Herman Melville said: "Life is a journey that is homeward bound."

When we leave her on her own today—her first real day of independence—my wife will have trouble holding back the tears, my son will want to get home to tape-measure his new room, and I'll drive home preoccupied with thoughts as to where the years have gone and how quickly our lives with our little girl have slipped by.

Like that prodigal son in the parable, my daughter has left home, but unlike him, my daughter won't hesitate to come back. We're rooted people, and our house will always be her home.

What we know and what we don't
October 9, 2006

When I think about the things of which I know virtually nothing, it scares me a little. I may know a few dates and facts in history, the names of my favorite books, and a line or two of poetry, but I really don't know near enough. Like many homeowners, I know how to replace a water heater and rewire a lamp, and I can hang mini-blinds without mashing a thumb. Much past that, and I'm a little iffy.

When I listen to music, say Vaughn Williams' 5th Symphony—one of my favorites—for instance, or even Eric Clapton do his thing on the guitar, I have no idea how people can make something that beautiful happen. Since I struggled with "Old King Cole" in an aborted attempt at playing the violin in sixth grade, I know I don't have a clue as to how people can make music in their heads, let alone how they write it down for others to play.

I can understand plinking out a tune on a piano with one hand; add the other hand and that's coordination that leaves me scratching my head. There are women at our churches who really know how to play the piano, but how they do it, I can't say. One friend, Kevin Hoggatt, played a beautiful piece at church a few months ago, and he "plays by ear." He can't read a note of music. How is that possible?

I know that when I see sculpture, perhaps something as wonderful as Daniel French's "Lincoln" or West

Terre Haute sculptor Bill Wolfe's work, I feel small because I struggled to make a decent-looking ashtray in seventh grade shop class. There is a magic in their hands that just isn't in mine, and good potters, pie-makers, and painters have the touch, too.

I used to spend a lot of time at Salty Seamon's art studio, and the stuff he threw in the trash after he showed me a little bit about shading or perspective or washing color was better than I could ever hope to do. He would sit at his painting table, a piece of paper anchored to it with masking tape, and create something where there was nothing before—a sycamore tree, a wheat field, a blackbird, a barn.

My friends Joe and Dennis can make a table, a baby's cradle, or a child's toy out of a few sticks of oak or sassafras; I admire that, and I've told them so. They may have degrees in mathematics, but they also see how to apply that subject to the building of a deck or the framing of a barn. What I may have half-way learned at a blackboard in school comes alive for them when cutting angles, figuring area, and making trim. They leave me smiling when I smell the wood and feel the grain of their labors.

My father-in-law, a retired farmer, never had much money in his life, but he's amazed me for years with his ability to keep old mechanical things going with little more than baling wire, spit, and a prayer. He understands how things work and begins tearing into them while I'm still looking at the operator's manual. He once completely dismantled a balky old lawn tractor of mine on my garage floor, tossing incomprehensible pieces into five-gallon buckets. After I ordered the part he said that I needed—waiting on it for weeks—he came back to that garage, dumped the parts on the floor, sat on the bucket, and put my tractor back together. I was impressed; he had nothing left over and that previous pile of oily parts was back to mowing my yard in a few hours. I'm also happy to know that my son, who spent much of his pre-school life with his grandpa, has a little of Gib's mechanical ability; it's going to come in handy someday.

I've often called one of my brothers-in-law to help me with electrical projects from time to time. Gene knows his stuff. What I assume or suspect will toast me on the spot, makes sense to him. I simply don't understand currents and resistance and figuring out exactly what I'm supposed to do with one of those little hand-held testers. He always seems to have an idea as to where I can start when solving a problem, just about the time I'm convinced I have no options.

My brother, John, has made canoes, rebuilt motor boats, built cabinets and bookcases, remodeled bathrooms, refinished furniture, tanned hides, and has become quite a good cook to boot. What he knows, he's learned by trial and error, by using his imagination, and by taking chances. I know I can do a few things he can't do, but I think I'd rather know more of what he can do than what I can.

A good teaching friend, Mike Hardesty, is a computer guru; the man simply knows things about computers that I can't fathom. I don't know the difference between a byte and megahertz, but Mike eats computer manuals like breakfast. If there's such a thing as technical common sense, he has it. He may swing a golf club like Fred Flintstone, but the man can scan, download, copy and paste, and transfer with the best of them. He's taught himself how to play the bagpipes and a half dozen other instruments too.

Over the years, I've come to marvel at what some folks can do. Emma Jean Jackson makes some of the best noodles I've ever had; Carol June Wiggins and my mom sat for hours hunched over ancient quilting frames and made quilts beautiful enough to call art; my wife can do the jumble we run in this newspaper faster than anyone on the planet. Phyllis Marsolf makes fantastic jelly; Dr. David Hay is a fine poet; Dan Collom built history with his hands at Bridgeton.

Because I have a couple of college degrees and a few pieces of paper that entitle me to be called educated, some people may think I'm pretty smart. But I think I have them fooled a little. I can plant a tree, do some basic plumbing, take a decent photograph, and quote Robert Frost. I was once told that I was good at trimming shrubs.

I'm smart all right; I know just enough to know that I don't know much at all.

Keep eyes open for life's "fabulous realities" January 1, 2007

It's been over 30 years since I first sat in Dr. James Mullican's composition class at Indiana State. I immediately liked the slow, somewhat southern lilt to his voice, his Icabod Crane-like gait, his intellect and kindness. I think I learned quite a bit about writing from him too.

My wife and I still see Dr. Mullican from time to time, at a library book sale or a play. He never fails to flash his toothy smile at us and say hello. He knows our affection for him was genuine, not a phony, please-raise-my-final-grade kind of friendliness.

Even though he obviously thought my wife, also a student in his grammar class, was the queen of commas and verb conjugation, which she most certainly is, and a favored student, which she also most certainly was, Dr. Mullican was perhaps the first person who ever told me that something I wrote was good. He also introduced me to something called "fabulous realities," a gift for which I will always be grateful.

Mullican was a great proponent of the writing guru Ken Macrorie, whose book, "Telling Writing," was used as the class's text. I still have my yellowing and dog-eared copy, now pushing 40 years old. In it, Macrorie emphasized his belief in the New English, a revolutionary approach to teaching writing in those days. He was also a great proponent of something he called "fabulous realities."

Fabulous realities just happen in life. As Macrorie said, "Most of us go through each day looking for what we saw yesterday and we find it, to our half-realized disappointment. But the man who daily expects to encounter fabulous realities runs smack into them again and again."

Macrorie wrote that fabulous realities are not "fairly surprising, but absolutely surprising, because they are unique." Dr. Mullican believed that too, and he encouraged us to keep a journal of them to help us get ideas for our writing. Much of what I write about in this column comes from my own fabulous realities lists, most often jotted down on anything I have at hand.

Macrorie listed several fabulous realities that his own students had seen: The girl who wore a particularly revealing blouse, yet held her books in front of herself in embarrassment; the sixteen-year-old kid who managed to buy a pack of cigarettes but couldn't resist five packs of bubble gum as well; the small boy who asked a department store security guard, "Did you see a lady walk by here without me?"

One of my favorite fabulous realities was a brief story about a man Macrorie mentioned who returned to his parked car to find its front end smashed and crumpled. On his windshield he found a neatly-folded piece of paper. Written in a feminine hand was a note that read, "I have just run into your car. There are people watching me. They think I am writing down my name and address. They are wrong."

Not a pleasant reality, but it was surprising.

In just the past few weeks I've noted a few fabulous realities of my own; noting them can be an addictive habit. For instance, I often get my morning cup of coffee at the drive-up window at the Clinton Dairy Queen before heading on to school. Just a few days ago, I had to wait for some unusual traffic to clear in front of me before I could get my cup filled. It wasn't cars that were holding me up, but rather two ducks, side-by-side, waddling their way past the pick-up window. They even paused near the intercom to quack their order. As I slowly idled toward my turn, I wondered where they kept their spare change.

Yet another fabulous reality came not long ago as I sat with my son on a cool Saturday afternoon watching a small-college football game. A young man walked by who looked like the Geico caveman, his hair a matted and dirty mess, his pants riding just low enough to spoil my anticipation of lunch. His school t-shirt simply read: "Add to the tradition."

Another fabulous reality came on Christmas morning as I watched my wife unwrap a glitzy and gilded package from Victoria's Secret. Out of the box came a long-sleeved flannel nightgown, more appropriate for "Little House on the Prairie" than "Sex in the City." The gift box was given to her for dramatic effect.

You know, if we take the time to do it, we really can see a lot of fabulous realities in our lives. Certainly, not all of them are welcomed, not all of them are funny either. But the surprise of seeing one does far more for me than supplying fodder for my column; it makes life more worth living.

I never mentioned it to Dr. Mullican, but when he asked us to make that master list of fabulous realities for good old English 307 years ago, I failed to mention one entry to him. While I saw so many of my professors drive their cars to campus and smugly park in a preferred and paved lot near the academic buildings, while we parked in muddy gravel and walked, I often saw one teacher who rode his bicycle, rain or shine, past me on 6th Street, his lunch and books riding in a basket on his handlebars. He often wore a rather unflattering fur cap, one in which the flaps could be unbuckled at its crown to be pulled down over its owner's cold, red ears.

The rider, his long legs pumping the pedals in the breeze, was Dr. Mullican. What a fabulous reality he is.

The day when 'stupid' brother borrowed a kite
March 26, 2007

I don't think it was the story I read in a grade school history book— complete with illustrations that showed a spindly-legged Benjamin Franklin flying a kite during a thunderstorm—that hooked me on kite flying at all. It was dirty soda pop bottles that did the trick.

When I was a kid I used to ride the hump-backed pavement of the Parke-Vigo County line road on my bicycle nearly every day of every summer, all the while keeping my eyes turned toward the ditches for pop bottles tossed out of passing cars by people who just didn't understand that they were throwing away real money. After all, the bounty for a returned bottle in those days was a hefty two cents, and if I was lucky, I could pick up just enough of them in the three miles between my house and Rosedale to earn an orange sherbet push-up or pack of baseball cards from Morgan's Variety Store.

Morgan's was a remarkably cool place for a kid. It was owned and operated by a pair of very nice people: Jess and Helen Morgan. Jess always wore white butcher's clothes and sported a nicely trimmed white mustache to match; he cut his own meat at the store. Helen wore bright red lipstick, had an incredibly high beehive hairdo that never seemed to move, and was inclined to call everyone in her store "Hon."

Morgan's Variety had it all: cloth to copper tubing, light bulbs to laxatives, socks to sandpaper. It smelled like dill and moth balls and powdered detergent. The Morgans also kept a barrel that in the spring sat next to the garden seed display. It always held a bundle of paper kites; their cost was 15 cents, or roughly seven-and-a-half ditched RC Cola bottles.

One spring day found my older brother, John, and me wandering the claustrophobic aisles of Morgan's deciding how to spend our ditch-digging bounty. I can't remember whether we sacrificed our Zero candy bars or red licorice whips or not, but we both managed to have enough cash to buy ourselves each a kite.

John, five years my senior, and very experienced in the art of intimidating a scrawny, freckle-faced punk like his brother, promptly snatched the only black pirate kite from the barrel. Its wrapping verified that it was not just any pirate kite either. It was the fulfillment of every kid's dream: to fly the Jolly Roger in all its evil glory in one's own back yard.

My kite was OK; it depicted a rather sissy-looking Casper the Friendly Ghost and was an odd shade of blue, but I could only see green as John handed over his money and banged through Morgan's screen door to his bicycle with that black skull and crossbones grinning at me through a clear plastic wrapper.

It took me no more than ten minutes after finishing my kite's assembly—which involved a careful trim job with my mom's sewing scissors, snapping two balsa wood supports into place, and adding a tail from the remnants of a shredded t-shirt—when I came through our backdoor sweating and bawling, Casper's face mutilated, not by a stout breeze, but rather by a failed attempt to ever get him into the air. Paper kites do not respond well to being dragged through the stubble of a soybean field.

In the meantime, John went on to smugly and successfully launch his kite with ease; I can still see it in its nefarious splendor, the Jolly Roger rattling in the wind at the end of two full lengths of kite string (a real wrist-building exercise since we hand-rolled our string onto sturdy sticks). After an arrogant maiden flight of a half-hour or so, John towed the pirate kite into harbor, checked it for any wear and tear, then promptly stored it along the stairwell that led into our basement. He then walked across the road to find my cousin, Roger, probably to chew on toothpicks or mess with a chemistry set.

I probably don't need to tell you that what happened next is one of the reasons why John flagged traffic down in front of our house for six months just to tell motorists how stupid his little brother was. I "borrowed" his kite, and, believe it or not, got the thing into the air with no damage whatsoever. That is until it became entangled in the high-tension transmission wires that hummed their way through the field just east of our house. I was lucky not to have been electrocuted, perhaps even luckier that my mom kept John from strangling me with the string left in my hands. The Jolly Roger flapped in the breeze until almost mid-summer, a grinning and faded reminder of my own slow-wittedness.

Over the years, I spent a lot of time flying kites with my own kids. I even went through a second childhood some time ago when I sent away for kite catalogues, and even bought one model that was nearly six feet across. I truly believe that apprenticing dads should take their kids fishing, build the occasional snowman, and hand down a fascination for kites to their children.

I've never really forgotten about the time I shanghaied my brother's Jolly Roger, and if you happen to see John, I think it's all right to bring the incident up now. Just don't ask him about the time I took his watch apart, okay?

Remembering Jim Jerome: One of the best men I ever knew April 23, 2007

There's a good chance that if you read this story, you're going to smile at least a little. It's about Jim Jerome, and if I knew him at all, I'd say smiling is what Jim most liked seeing people do.

Jim died late last month at 81. He hadn't grasped his mike nor eyeballed his stat sheet, hadn't carried on his customary commercial break banter with passers-by or opened a radio broadcast with his trademark "Hi everybody!" for years, but Jim was special to folks in Parke and Vermillion counties, special to anyone who met him.

A typical story about Jim comes from a cold January night some 25 years ago. Jerome, WAXI's bi-county high school play-by-play man, sat shoulder-to-shoulder amid an overflow crowd in a steamy Rosedale gymnasium calling a game between the Hotshots and dreaded rival Rockville. The hosts were down at least 30 points, but Jim never lost his touch, calling the action as if the game was going down to the wire.

During a commercial break, a lady who had been listening to Jim and partner Charlie Bemis most of the night, tapped him on the shoulder and asked, "Are you broadcasting this game?"

Bemis, Jerome's alter-ego on the air for 21 years, said

it best in the eulogy he delivered at Jim's memorial service on April 14, and to me on the telephone last week: "Jim was so happy doing those games. He never wanted any of our kids to lose. He loved the grassroots kind of games at places like Montezuma and Rosedale and Rockville and Turkey Run. The games were exciting, and every once in a while they were even close."

Jim covered his first basketball game in the winter of 1950 for WFMU out of Crawfordsville. By the time he hung up the microphone in 1998, he was an institution. "He was the best interview guy in the world," Bemis said. "We were able to meet so many neat people through basketball and football games, and Jim just smiled through the whole thing. He never met a stranger."

I can attest to that; the first time I met Jim I was a 24-year-old varsity basketball coach who handled an open microphone like it was radioactive. I began to sit in with Jim and a half-dozen other coaches on his "Saturday Sidelines" show, and I was sure he must have thought me at first to be a dim bulb. It became a bit uncomfortable for me when he would ask me a question, then expect me to talk long enough for him to swallow a half a cup of coffee, finish off his bacon and eggs, or run to the restroom.

It wasn't hard to find Jim around town; the man kept busy. He was a bank vice-president, a journalist, was a master of ceremonies for just about every queen contest and pie judging contest in the county, led tours at the historical museum, acted with the Parke Players, and worked quietly behind the scenes for the Lions Club and the Junior Chamber of Commerce. Jim wasn't just a good man; he was a good citizen. He served in the Army Air Corps during World War II; he helped found Billie Creek Village.

Despite owning a resume that would have sent other folks in search of bigger hats, Jim never lost his self-deprecating humor. Bemis related a story about a time he, Jim, and friend Larry Gambiani posed at the RCA Dome with "Sports Goofy," for a picture that Jim proudly displayed.

"You know why I love that photo?" he would tell his friends. "It's the only picture I have where somebody in it has a bigger nose than me," he'd say, then undoubtedly follow the comment with that big, genuine laugh of his.

Years ago, I sat down with Jim at his home for iced tea and sports talk. We ambled through his house, looked through an overflowing filing cabinet, thumbed through old scorebooks, looked at pictures, shared a few stories. He told me that it had been a long time since 1950, that he'd had a good life, that he'd met a lot of nice people through his job.

When I left three hours later, I was amazed that he had never really made it in the big-time with a bigger radio station, had not had an even bigger following. The man had called games from Market Square Arena, the RCA Dome, Hulman Center, and the beautiful relic of Butler Fieldhouse. He had been honored by the

IHSAA with a Distinguished Service Award, and, along with Bemis, had been named a Sagamore of the Wabash. But he also told me that day, "I've always lived in my own little world: small towns and small schools."

Small towns and small schools maybe; big-time, nonetheless.

Depending on the kindness of friends
July 30, 2007

I have been searching off and on in my filing cabinets these past few weeks for a favorite column by Ernie Pyle. In it, he wrote of a return trip to his hometown of Dana after years on the road. His mother had suffered a stroke, and when he came into his home place, he saw the pots and covered dishes that neighbors and friends had brought in to help feed his parents in their time of need.

He was not only impressed with the charity of his parents' friends, but he also recalled the times when he saw his mother preparing and taking food to sick neighbors. She often volunteered to supply a meal after a funeral or at some other time of crisis, so her friends were simply returning the kindness that she had offered to them; it was the right thing to do.

That scenario has been played out in my household in the past few weeks. And it suddenly made me understand that kindness and charity are not dead, at least not in my community and among my friends and family.

My wife recently had surgery, and after four days in uncharacteristic inactivity in a hospital bed, she arrived home to recuperate. I was concerned that I couldn't do an adequate job of taking care of her, particularly when it came to cooking decent meals.

After all, despite slurping down her home-cooked fare without taking a breath, my idea of good food when left on my own is canned chili or a few bowls of cereal, maybe an English muffin.

I really shouldn't have been concerned about feeding her, and my son, who when hungry—which is most of the time—is a 6'5" harvesting machine who cuts a swath of culinary destruction before him. He often hits our refrigerator like a swarm of locusts, leaving empty milk jugs and flaccid shrink wrap in his wake.

Doing the dishes and sweeping the floors was within my domestic grasp, but actually preparing a reasonable meal, other than bacon and eggs, was a leap I didn't think I could make. As it turned out, I didn't really have to.

On the first evening my wife was home, our good friend, Linda Huxford, brought in a feast. Her Italian beef and brownies with chocolate icing left me with a job of no more than cleaning up microwavable dishes and wiping out her food basket. Leftovers took care of lunch for two more days.

On the second night, Madonna Ball continued the pattern of best friends' wives doing the cooking and delivering by bringing in lasagna, green beans, and a pan of cookie bars—she knows no one else in my family probably saw many of those—that once again supplied dinner and a few subsequent lunches.

Our third evening meal was to be supplied by a good friend of my wife. Kelley Webb is among a tight little group of school friends my wife meets with about once a month for a ladies' night out, and she volunteered to swing by a spaghetti place to pick up our supper.

She never made it out of Terre Haute; her car was broadsided just before she got to the restaurant's parking lot. She was subsequently laid up for a few days herself, but my wife couldn't take a meal in for her. Pardon the paraphrase, but there's no greater friend than one who would lay down her own automobile to help another...

The next guest chef was my mother-in-law, Pat Dickey. I have been eating off her table for 30 years now, and each of us anticipated amounts and varieties of food that we have come to love. Pat has never believed that sugar and real butter and gravy are bad for you, so we got pretty substantial dollops of all those with her pork cutlets, home-canned corn, and peach pie. I think we just emptied the last containers of her leftovers a few nights ago.

Within another day, Sue Weber, another of my wife's good buddies, brought over a banquet worthy of Nebuchadnezzar: chicken, baked beans, cheese potatoes, garlic toast, salad, and an ice cream/Oreo cookie dessert, that to put it mildly, is one of the best things life can offer. Sadly, I later learned that on the night my family enjoyed that repast, Sue's husband, Dennis, was left home alone to dine on frozen pizza. I felt guilty the next night, for about five minutes, as we finished off the dessert.

The next day, my sister-in-law, Karen Baxter, brought us both a nice spinach dip and an angel food cake. On another night they blended nicely with a few things my wife had tucked away in the freezer before she went to the hospital. On the heels of that, yet another sister-in-law, Terri Nepote, truly delivered. Just a few months ago, I drove my wife to Terri's to take her family a pan of lasagna after she too had been in the hospital for a few days—brother-in-law, Dom, was seen waiting at the picture window like a hungry housecat—and Terri reciprocated with a wonderful meal of steak and potatoes and strawberry pie. I still have pleasant dreams about that pie.

My wife is feeling much better now; against my advice, she plans to begin washing the house today. She's undoubtedly recovering faster than her doctors thought she would, which has been a blessing in more than one way.

You see, last week we started remodeling our eyesore of a kitchen, along with a small bathroom and laundry area too. We are living the nomadic life of the displaced, eating off a card table in our family room, using a toaster that sits on the floor, and washing dishes in our bathroom sink. She's been a real trooper through it all.

Just when I thought the spoiling of that neighborly charity had ebbed, particularly since we have been using paper plates and eating out of a mini-refrigerator for a while, a friend of ours from church, Carmen Palma, called.

"I know your kitchen is wrecked," she said, "so Jerry (Carmen's husband, who's no stranger to her cooking talent) and I thought we'd bring a meal over for you Monday evening, if that would be alright."

I had the card table all set up, but sadly, Jerry fell ill and Carmen couldn't make it. I'll bet someone takes food in for them though. Believe me, the spirit of Ernie Pyle's mother lives on.

Duty done, soldiers came home to build communities October 8, 2007

As I sat back to watch a little of Ken Burns' epic documentary about World War II last week, I couldn't help but think of a great uncle I never met. Albert Lunsford wasn't yet 26 when he was killed near Hagenau, France in January 1945. Albert never came home; he was buried in an American cemetery near Epinal.

Albert's son, Gene, came to live with my grandparents after his dad was lost, and my dad became more like a brother to him than a cousin; my Grandfather Roy and Grandmother Blanche were happy to take him in, and to this day, whenever I see Gene, he wants to talk about Dad and my grandparents.

My uncle was one of ten Gold Star boys from Parke

County in World War II. I don't suppose he was a whole lot unlike Sergeant Joseph Beal, a gunner on a B-17 who was lost in 1943, or PFC John Lewis Howard, who was killed in action near Cassano, Italy in 1944. They were all young, like Sgt. Robert Trout, who died with the 43rd Infantry on Luzon, and 1st Lt. Victor Hartman, who was lost in the Pacific war. Both were only 26.

I don't want to be too hard on my generation, but it's not an overstatement to say that most aging Boomers like me have had no task in our lives as intimidating as the invasion of Fortress Europe or the island-hopping campaign that American fighting men tackled at Peleliu and Iwo Jima and Okinawa; we should be grateful for that. It sure looks more and more like our children, and perhaps their children, are going to have their work cut out for them in places like Iraq and Afghanistan fighting people every bit as evil as Hitler and Tojo.

While I watched one of Burns' episodes last week in my cramped office at home, I spied a book my brother-in-law, Gene Baxter, gave to me a few years ago. Knowing that I'm a nostalgic packrat, he thought of me after he'd found a box of old books in an attic.

Among the dusty texts and novels he delivered was a book called "Parke County in The World War." Published in 1920 by the Rockville Tribune, it is a wonderful tribute to the men who served in the Great War, the war that was supposedly fought to prevent the even bigger one that came 20 years later and killed

Albert and Corporal Ken Haas and Pvt. Harold Hart, and Lester Montgomery, who died in the fighting near the Douves River. They too were all from my county.

There's no way I would have known that they'd been "Over There," of course, but as a kid I knew a few of the men pictured in that book. For instance, Dee Cottrell, the local undertaker in Rosedale for years, was in it; he took care of the arrangements for all of my grandparents. Glennie Williams is in the book too; I had his grandkids in my classroom, but I knew him only as an old, old man. He looks so young in the picture—probably taken in 1918—with his high white starched collar appearing to stretch his neck.

The family names in that book remind me that many of those men came back to Parke County and made lives for themselves. Its pages are filled with pictures of Crookses and Cases, Hobsons and Hartmans, Welches and Woodards.

Perhaps even more of a connection for me is a service record of the Rosedale community from both world wars that Milbrey Huxford loaned to me a while ago. Her husband, Wayne, was a gunner in the war, and he, and a lot of other men I know, or once knew, is in that book. My great uncles are pictured there: Uncle Will and Uncle Bob and Uncle Tom, and Albert. My aunt's husband, Gilbert "Bub" Herzog is there too. He saw Hitler's Eagle's Nest and came home to be a truck driver. My Great Aunt Alice's husband, Everett Allen, is there. He was a very quiet man, a pipe-smoking farmer; he fought in the Rhineland.

Bill Engle is in the book too. It took a number of years of attending church with Bill before I ever knew that he had fought in Europe; he was awarded a Bronze Star. The Howk brothers—Dick and Ron—are there, and so are Bob Montgomery and Perry Huxford; I still see those guys from time to time, and each is a gentleman.

Many of the faces on those pages are of men I knew: Sandy Crowder and George Dean, Jess Morgan, Hubert Brown and Ralph Harrison, Roy Hastings and Bob "Goose" Yowell all served during WWII but are gone now. So are Walt Williams, my childhood mail carrier, and Freeman and Bob Chaney; they owned the property I now call home.

Hubert McHargue came home to be a school teacher and basketball coach at Rosedale. Not many years ago I sat in his living room and talked late into the night about his teams. Bob McPike often waved to me as he sat on his front step and I jogged by his house. Everett Newton, who lived just a few miles down the road, is in the book, too; his picture is as impressive as a Marine Corps recruitment poster. Roy Tolin owned a farm just a stone's throw from my in-laws' place; he had a beautiful brick home. Jack Williams is there, too; he came to be a dear friend of ours. And, Bill Baxter, Gene's dad, is there; he fought in the Ardennes and was awarded a Purple Heart and a Silver Star.

I know I've undoubtedly left some men out. The book is filled with Rukeses and Jukeses, with McMullens and Magers, and Pralls and Perrys. I apologize in advance for the oversight.

Early each year in my history class, I teach the old basic economic principle of TANSTAAFL—"There ain't no such thing as a free lunch." It was true in the days of the Old West when sandwiches lured men and their thirsts into competing saloons, and I hope my students understand that it remains true now in a much larger sense.

Somehow, somewhere, folks like me are enjoying freedoms that men like the ones I've just mentioned paid for. The least we can do is thank them for it.

A gift to others proved to be one to myself
October 22, 2007

After my mom died a few years ago, my sister and brother and I were forced to hastily clean her things from the apartment in which she lived after illness had moved her into town from her country home. Because we were trying to vacate the place as quickly as we could, it was one of my jobs to haul a wicker box of photographs out to my car. It has been stored in a backroom closet since the day I brought it home.

At our last family reunion, my sister and brother-in-law mentioned the box, hoping that I'd get it out so that my niece, Sarah, could look through it for photos of her and her grandmother. In fact, we decided that this winter we'd get together and go through the box, maybe at Thanksgiving. We know it will bring memories flooding back to us, and I expect more than a few laughs—perhaps even a few tears—in the process.

I hadn't really looked through the treasure trove much. Mom was pretty good about writing on the backs of old photos, but I know there will be a number of pictures of folks who will remain forever unidentified, suspended in their rectangular black-and-white and gray worlds unless my brother or sister knows who they are.

This story will serve as a spoiler for my family, but in the interim, I decided to take a few pictures that Mom gave to me years ago, pull a few more from that box, and use a scanner—one of our age's great inventions—to put together what I hope will be a gift that will be appreciated: a compact disk of old pictures that they'll be able to thumb through or print as they see fit.

In that process, however, I ended up giving myself more pleasure than anything I've done in a long time. My mom was no scrapbooker; pictures she deemed worthy of being kept went into the box. There was no order, no elaborate decorative scheme, but that proved to be a beautiful thing because at each layer of the box came surprises.

One of the first pictures I discovered was of Mom, herself, perhaps at 11 or 12. She is standing next to her bicycle, two small terriers perched in a basket mounted over her front wheel. A caption in faded ink hints that one of the dogs was named Louie. It is odd to see your parents at such a young ages; their lives were still in front of them.

Next, I found a photo of my great aunt, Lillian Lane, and her husband, Arlo. They too are very young—perhaps their mid-20s—and she is smartly dressed in pleated skirt, black hosiery and stylish shoes; Arlo wears a vest and has a shining buckle on his belt. I can only remember them as an older couple who lived out by the strip mines of Sandford. My uncle was nearly bent in half at the waist after he had broken his back in the mines, and I used to explore his barn lot, run from his goats, and sit on his ancient Silver King, spitting out tractor noises and cranking its steering wheel. Lillian was nicknamed "Dingy," affectionately so because of her wonderful sense of humor, and I loved our visits there.

I soon found a photo of my brother. In it he stands next to a tricycle; he is dressed in bibbed overalls, and just behind him is a concrete block retaining wall that my dad built near our house. What would become the back yard I knew is little more than a brushy patch yet to be cleared; a bit of my grandparents' house peeks through trees.

Next, I discovered a picture of my grandfather, Roy, one of his brothers, Bob, and my dad; they had been fishing, and my grandpa mugs for the camera, a string of fish in his left hand, while Bob looks straight into the camera, and Dad laughs at his dad, his thick, freckled fingers resting on his hips. A photograph later and Dad is shown sitting on our scratchy, gray couch. My brother, at five, is smiling in his striped shirt with fancy snaps, and my sister, about two, sits on my dad's left leg and appears to have been startled by the flash. I am positioned on the other leg, clueless and grinning in a bib and diaper.

A sepia-toned picture caught my eye next; it was nearly eight inches wide, but only three inches tall, and in it 20 or so students, perhaps eighth-graders or freshmen in high school, sit at heavy desks and stare at the camera. Barely noticeable in the lower right-hand corner is an arrow pointing to a pretty, dark-haired girl, her chin resting on her hand. My mother had written "Mom" beneath her, and it wasn't hard then to see my grandmother sitting there, although she had years to go before she met John Hill and married him. It must have been 1926 or so, and several of the girls had bobbed hair. Most of the boys appear to have never had a comb.

In one of my favorite pictures, nine of us, including my dad and cousin, Roger, sit in folding lawn chairs, huge slabs of watermelon tucked below our gaping mouths. We are eating near Taylor's Pond, one of our favorite summertime haunts. Joe Taylor, a school buddy of Dad's, would often have us over to fish and gab. We'd fill a wash tub with pop and roast hot dogs over a fire and only leave when the sun dipped below the tree line.

My mom kept a bushel of photos, some old, some not so old. In one of them, my own family sits along a rock wall overlooking the waters of Sugar Creek; the maples are just showing a hint of gold behind us. I have my arms wrapped around my son, his hair buzzed in a crew cut. My daughter, who had yet to finish high school, sits next to her mother. It was just eight years ago, but so much has happened since then...

It's amazing that a grown man can take a journey in a small wicker box.

Getting ready to play in the biggest game of all November 19, 2007

In many ways, Justin McLaughlin was one of the most frustrating students I've ever had. I say that because despite trying just about everything on him in class except a cattle prod, Justin just didn't much see the point of wasting valuable time studying spelling and writing and reading. After all, he had turkeys to hunt, fish to catch, girls to charm, and running backs to tackle. You practically had to tie the kid in his chair to keep him in the room. He was a bundle of energy that only paintball or wrestling or horsing around with pals could curb.

Justin was a typical high school kid. He undoubtedly wore one of the grubbiest ball caps I have ever seen, loved to fish—sometimes at the expense of attending class altogether—and often got more than a little sleepy while we discussed common and proper nouns or Ernest Hemingway.

He also played a little basketball for me. I unretired myself from coaching just long enough to take on the seventh and eighth grade boys' teams at the time that Justin and his buddies were coming through the program, and despite missing his seventh grade year after blowing out a knee playing football, by eighth grade he had convinced his mom and dad that he wanted to play hoops, so out he came to play dragging a bulky knee brace that was wrapped around his leg like a bird cage.

What may have frustrated me the most about this guy was the fact that despite his resistance to reading a good book or memorizing even a single line of poetry, or even faking that he enjoyed a short story, I liked him, and he knew it. I liked him because he was funny and kind, and he always said "Morning" to me as he walked to his desk like a man going to the gallows. I liked him because I knew that underneath that Huck Finn sort of veneer he had, Justin was, and is a friend.

Now, I don't mean to speak about Justin in the past tense at all. The last time I saw him was in July at a farewell party at his parents' home out on the County Line Road. He was headed to Army boot camp, and his family and friends were both happy to be together, yet more than a little sad to see him go. There were a ton of hugs and a gallon of tears handed out that day, and more than a few of them came from that tough kid himself.

Justin may not have found his calling in my English classroom, but in the Army he has been as comfortable as that crusty old cap of his. He had his basic training at Fort Benning, Georgia as a member of the Infantry's Bravo unit and came out in the top five of his recruiting class of 59. Out of the 202 soldiers that Justin went into camp with, he was one of a handful who was asked to join the elite Army Rangers. He became squad leader when the original leader didn't meet expectations, and now he's to report to Fort Hood, Texas pretty soon. From there he'll head to Iraq in December.

It's a big leap to take from driving an old blue pick-up to a local fishing hole to leading men into combat. And it has to be frightening to know that one minute you've got your girl by the arm at the senior prom, and the next you're covering your buddy's back in Baghdad. But apparently that's exactly what Justin wants to do; he volunteered for active duty.

I remember that I spent hours with that boy trying to get him to learn how to block off for a rebound or to get his elbow in under his jump shot. I also remember that Justin was one player that I could depend on; he didn't care about scoring, wasn't worried about ever being a star and racking up impressive stats. He just wanted to be on the team and have fun.

Well, now Justin is on another team, and I hope it's one that's well coached, because much more than cutting down a championship net is at stake. If I know Justin like I think I do, the Army has a real live wire on its hands. Just don't ask him to work on vocabulary words or sentence fragments.

You know, when I coached Justin years ago, or had him in class, or watched him play in the navy, burgundy, and white with my son on the football field, a lot of people used to "pray" that his knee would hold up or he'd remember an in-bounds play, or that he'd even be ready for his literature test. But praying then was mostly a figure of speech.

It needs to be the real deal now.

Sitting and listening to the "speech of the angels" December 3, 2007

I sat in the comforting darkness of the Tilson Auditorium balcony a few weeks ago, my wife and daughter to my left and the soft glow of the stage lights below me. We were there to take in a performance of the Terre Haute Symphony Orchestra and its guest pianist, Di Wu.

Ask anyone who knows me, and I think they would tell you that I enjoy all kinds of music. I have a favorite oldies radio station tuned in while I drive, and I own a pretty decent collection of jazz and easy listening and classic rock and pop; I even take an interest in what my 20-year-old son is listening to from time to time.

But classical is at the top of my list. I know I'm a novice, someone who has to read heavily in the program notes to come close to understanding what I am hearing, but I know what I like, and thankfully I was turned on to classical music when I was young, and I've never lost my interest in it.

I grew up in a home where music was an essential. We had a stereo in our living room, and right along with our Lefty Frizzel and Patsy Cline albums was a big collection of classical excerpts that my mom picked up at the S&H Green Stamps store. It wasn't exactly season tickets to the New York Philharmonic, but it was enough to pique an interest in a kid who had already tried and miserably failed to make his mother happy by playing the violin, which certainly looked easier than it was.

I want to apologize right now to my first music teacher, Evelyn Vaught. Mrs. Vaught sweat bullets for me; she believed I could play the violin. In special lessons in the quiet of her big Collett Park home, she labored with me as if I were a prodigy, often sitting at her piano bench, wondering, I'm sure, if I was really trying at all. She came to our house on Saturdays, and she spent extra time with me at school, too; I'll never forget the little pitch pipe she carried in her pocket, or the autoharp she took to our classrooms. Mrs. Vaught was just about the kindest person I had ever met, but I knew even then that I was destined to let her down. After just a few months of fighting and cajoling and pleading with me, my mom tearfully returned my rented violin to the store and bought me a pair of high-top basketball shoes.

I believe that my interest in classical music got jump-started on a rainy day when I was in the fifth grade, a year before I tried to tackle violin lessons. It was on days like those that Miss Gardner, our diminutive and sometimes too-cheery physical education teacher—who I believe could actually bend at the waist and touch the floor with her elbows—came to our room pushing an old brown tabletop record player. She used to force us to spend rainy days learning to dance, which is a particularly abhorrent thing when one is in fifth grade and has no interest in even touching a girl, let alone dancing with one.

But on that memorably wet October afternoon Miss Gardner brought in a worn and scratchy LP of Camille Saint-Saens' "Danse Macabre," a rather creepy little tone poem meant to interest us as we neared the Halloween season. I must say, it did the trick. Saint-Saens's ghoulish violinist and bone-like xylophone really touched me, and I think I have been a fan of the classical genre ever since.

By seventh grade, I was introduced to the decidedly non-academic side of junior high school scheduling: Music Appreciation. My school offered band, vocal, and orchestral programs, but a hearty, and I'm sure somewhat unmotivated gang of us who didn't wish to try an instrument or "train" our voices, headed off to one corner of the school auditorium every day to learn something about music, lest we be less cultured than those who were tooting their horns and lugging their cellos around. And I am very thankful for it, too.

It was in Music Appreciation that I met Eugene Esperson, a wonderful amalgam of old school discipline and wise-cracking practical joker dressed in a tie and tweed jacket. He had a pretty tough job, but in my case, he certainly held his own. Every day we went to Music Appreciation and listened to Esperson's ancient collection of records and studied the rudiments of music. I know he had to find us to be musical dunces, but he endured it, and it was because of him that I came to love Gershwin's "Rhapsody in Blue" and Ravel's "Bolero," even a little opera.

High School was more about Don Mclean and REO Speedwagon and Led Zeppelin and The Moody Blues, a decidedly confused and eclectic period in music, but by college I was once again back in a general education music appreciation class, listening to Zoltan Szabo's lectures on Gregorian Chants, the Romantic Movement and Beethoven, and the harsh dissonance of Bela Bartok. I found myself in the balcony of Tilson Auditorium, too, glad to have a free student pass to the concerts.

In that wonderful nest I heard the glories of Vaughn Williams and Tchaikovsky and Mozart, and years after my college days were over, I just kept going back for more. I was there to see the immortal Aaron Copland the night the orchestra performed his "Fanfare for a Common Man;" was there when a very young Joshua Bell soloed; was there when pianist Lorin Hollander held the audience spell-bound with Rachmaninoff's "Rhapsody on a Theme by Paganini," then returned to the stage two more times to play encores. I saw the tears running down his face as he played a piece by Bach—his father's favorite. I don't believe I will ever forget that moment.

I'm here to tell you that you need not be a longhair, an academic, or a bluenose to enjoy the symphony;

music is music. Bruce Springsteen says that the "best music is essentially there to provide you with something to face the world with." Long-dead critic Thomas Carlyle put it even more perfectly. He believed that music "is well said to be the speech of angels."

One night, years ago, as I sat in the balcony at Tilson just before the lights began to fade and the concert was to begin, I saw a tall, reed-thin woman make her way to a seat in front of me near the railing. I knew, despite the distance between us, that it was Evelyn Vaught.

When I stepped down to see her, she called out my name, remembering me through all the years. Surely, I was one of her worst students, but typically, she was gracious and kind and genuinely happy to see me.

Now, I can't help but think of her every time I sit in the darkness of that place, just before the bows touch the strings.

CHAPTER TWO

PLACES

Making an argument for staying put
July 18, 2005

I've had a number of people ask me why I've stayed put so long; why I haven't moved to a different job, bought a newer house, gone on to a bigger town. I usually answer with a stock response: I'm in a place where I feel I am supposed to be.

In his wonderful travelogue, "Blue Highways," the author, who took his father's Native American name, William Least Heat Moon, describes a night he spent sitting at the kitchen table with an aged couple in the backwoods of Tennessee. He wrote that it was "one of those sweet moments that I knew would stay with me forever." In other words, it was one of those perfect instances that make us content and happy.

I've had that feeling many times myself in the place in which I've chosen to live, with the people I've chosen to live with. It may have been at the end of a day's work, and I looked toward the sun's dying glow in the west over a field of clipped grass; it may have come to me as I sat in the early morning of a summer day, a cup of coffee and a crossword on my desk as both the birds and my house woke from their sleep. It may have come in the cool darkness of a movie theater as my wife sat next to me quietly sobbing over the triumphs of a horse judged too old and too small to win, silently glad that through her tears she couldn't see that my eyes were a little bleary too.

I've heard that moment in a Mozart concerto, seen it

in a Rockwell painting, felt it in my hand as I rolled a stone worn smooth by a creek's persistence, smelled it when the April breeze blew out of the north and through the locust tree grove that runs along our yard. I think if we listen and look long enough, quietly enough, we'll all have those moments.

Do we live in a world where people are too caught up with getting ahead to realize that what they're searching for may already be at hand? I plead guilty to ambition myself, but as I age, I get a bit more comfortable with being in my own skin, with the crack in the living room ceiling, with owning cars with odometers ready to begin their lives again, with a roll-top desk piled high with bits and pieces of my life stuck into its nooks and crannies. Ambition is fine, but it may very well lead us away from the things and people that, in the long run, matter the most to us.

I haven't just begun to ponder these things; in many ways, I think I've always been a homebody, happy that I have a sanctuary to return to, where it is quiet and comfortable, where blue jeans and home-grown tomatoes and home-cooked meals have always been and still are the order of the day.

Several years ago, I met the essayist Scott Russell Sanders, an Indiana University writing professor whose books about home and family have helped me realize just how fortunate I am to live where I live, and that staying here isn't about weakness and conformity, but rather about the strength of conviction. In fact, Sanders wrote a book called "Staying Put: Making a

Home in a Restless World;" I return to its pages often. Sanders is a quiet man, an intelligent man, a man who could live and prosper anywhere in the country, but he chooses to continue to live in southern Indiana. It's his home.

In an essay called "Settling Down," Sanders recalls the story of a family of childhood neighbors, the Millers. Over the span of just a few years three different tornadoes struck their Ohio farm, and after each one, the family rebuilt. They had made a commitment to the place they called home, and they intended to stick to it.

Sanders writes, "These tornado memories dramatize a choice we are faced with constantly: whether to go or to stay, whether to move to a situation that is safer, richer, easier, more attractive, or to stick where we are and make what we can of it. . .There are voices enough, both inner and outer, urging us to deal with difficulties by pulling up stakes and heading for new territory."

Perhaps I should have started with what brought this piece to mind: a front page table of statistics printed in the Tribune-Star a week or two ago that showed that most of the small towns and rural counties that we call the Wabash Valley are losing people, not gaining them, that folks are fleeing this place—or at least not coming here—because jobs are few and far between, because crime is growing worse, because our schools' test scores aren't high enough. There's a litany of reasons.

Just last week, midway through a day spent with a friend of mine pooling our labor to cut a dying tree at his house and to spread a few tons of white rock at mine, we stopped at a local restaurant for lunch. Our waitress was a girl who years ago sat in my history classroom. We talked about the small town in which she was raised. She doesn't live there anymore; it's changed, she says, for the worse. It's dying, but she wishes that it could be like it once was.

She hasn't gone far though, and perhaps if more of us stay put, and fight the good fight, we'll have something worth staying for.

Feeding my friend, Simon
August 13, 2005

A buddy of mine says that in a few more years, he will retire and probably move, perhaps nearer to Indianapolis where he can live closer to malls and restaurants and his two girls. Although I understand his wanting to locate nearer to the latter of the three, I can't say much in support of the first two.

My wife and I love living in the country. Besides, a friend of ours joins us for dinner every night, and he needs us here.

That friend is a possum who pokes around in a compost pile of leftover table scraps just over our back hillside. He became a regular last summer and we took to calling him Simon, a name my wife lifted from a series of mystery novels by Rita Mae Brown.

Simon is a most accommodating fellow, and like his fictitious brother in Brown's books, he gladly shares his table with our four nosey cats and any other hungry forest friend who happens to crawl or walk by. It's not unusual to see him scurrying around the watermelon rinds and brown lettuce, running his pale snout over bones picked clean of meat, accidentally pulling his grimy tail through stale crackers and old cereal. He really is into what he eats, and like all of his possum pals, his cuteness lies in his ugliness.

Occasionally, Simon will wander up to our back deck for a bite of the food we leave out during the day for our cats, but for the most part, he just waits along our wood line for his dinner, knowing that as soon as we finish our supper near dusk, he'll get his soon enough. He doesn't even hiss at us anymore, knowing we have no intention of domesticating him or turning him into some sort of hideous lap dog.

My wife and I, and our two kids, have lived in the country all our lives. We have often said that the only place we could be induced to move to would be one that is farther out into the woods, away from the stoplights and too-loud car stereos and factory smells. Besides the quiet, it's visitors like Simon who keep us here.

I think we have raised our children to respect living things, and we've been rewarded through the years by dozens of encounters, most of them welcomed, by the things that live in our trees, burrow into our hills, patrol our skies, and occasionally drink from our hoses.

My wife religiously feeds the hummingbirds, and each spring we are rewarded with a larger crop of the needle-nosed busybodies who peek in our picture windows and expect their daily sugar fix from our stovetop. We've also heard and watched the red-tailed hawks as they soar over the valley to the east of our house, and once last year, I stood in my office doorway and watched as one majestically perched not 30 feet away from my step to either sit and watch a potential meal or to show off his rust-colored tail. Nearly every day we can stand in our yard and watch a Great Blue Heron purposefully fly over our house, or hear a trio or two of Canada geese as they make their daily runs from the pond below our hill to one a mile west, honking as if to clear the air of oncoming traffic. In the summer afternoons, we often catch sight of a blue-tailed skink tanning itself on the woodpile near our door.

A half-dozen summers ago, my family watched a box turtle drop her load of thin-shelled white eggs, perhaps seven or eight of them, into a shallow hole she had dug in our yard near a clump of peonies. It was a place that I had mowed every week until she decided to turn it into her nursery. For weeks, we waited and watched until her children emerged from the dirt to march toward the woods in a solemn procession.

My kids have been privileged to grow up, like I did just a few miles away, in a place where they can see brown rabbits snooping behind our barn or among the honeybees and dragonflies in our flower garden, coal black and red-yellow milk snakes slithering through our yard or coiled in the sun on a rock wall, and deer as they pop out of a neighboring cornfield near sundown to cross the road. A few years ago we all stood a respectful distance from a speckled fawn as it lay against one of our fences, tired and confused until it figured out a way to get under the wire and into a grove of shingle oaks with its mother.

To be sure, some of our wild friends aren't always welcomed guests. The field mice do their best to run amok in my barn, and occasionally a kitchen cabinet. The black snakes have invaded us from our attic. The raccoons raid our squirrel corn and bird feeders and cat dishes. I gave up trying to grow much more than tomatoes because the rabbits used my vegetable garden as their own private buffet.

But their intrusions, along with the hornets who build paper nests along my gutters, the bats who creepily hang in the hayloft, and the moles that bulldoze my yard, are the price we pay for living among the living. I've had snakes fall into my lap from trees, raccoons snap at my hands from live traps, and sparrows build nests in our front porch hanging pots, but I've come to accept them all as neighbors.

Of all the animals we cohabitate with, I'd have to say that among our favorites are the little green and brown tree frogs that we find plastered to our house at night, their sticky little feet palming our siding like basketballs as they hang around a porch light or doorway slurping down gnats and moths as fast as I do my wife's cookies.

A few summers ago, one of the frogs took up residence in one of our bluebird boxes. We'd see him proudly perched in the opening every day, the sole inhabitant of his own frog condo. It is always a true sign of an oncoming spring when we hear the little peepers near the pond in March, crawling from the ooze to let us know they've made it through the winter, too.

There's more to tell—stories about butterflies drawn to our black-eyed Susans, the wild turkeys that waltz across our back yard, the foxes we've seen run across the road, the groundhog we have along one hillside that shows his face and grunts at us every month or two.

Often, we just hear these neighbors crashing through the woods as they hear our approach, or we shake them loose from hiding as we reach for a raspberry or mushroom. But they're here, and as long as we can take care of our home, we are, too.

My wife asked me yesterday about a spot in our yard where I saw a painted turtle deposit four or five eggs in June. It is unusual to see them away from the pond and in the arid brown grass of open spaces, but nonetheless, she was there. According to a field guide we often use, the eggs should be hatching soon, maybe this week. We don't know if they will ever break the soil's surface, or if once they do, they stand much of a chance of surviving their caravan to a wet log or stagnant pool. We just wanted to see them before they left.

In the meantime, Simon is in for a feast tonight. My wife is cleaning out the refrigerator.

Paying attention to the sounds of silence
October 24, 2005

Anyone who knows my wife and me also knows that we walk or bike the roads around our home place like we own them. I don't think that most people think that the two of us could possibly be entertained much anymore by looking at the same landscape, the same houses, the same fields and barns and ditches and patches of woods virtually every day, but they'd be wrong. It's odd, but somehow, we always seem to see something different each day, something subtly changed, some new shade or shadow or view.

The pavement we most often walk was once called Snow Road. Whether it was given that name for its notorious January drifts, or perhaps for Maude Snow, who years ago lived at its end, we're not sure. Either way, it's now been blandly given a number in a system that few really seem to understand, and I find that most folks who have lived here long still refer to it by its antiquated name.

The wind has taken a U-turn these past few weeks, and as the trees begin their colorful changes and the sun slips a little lower in the west a bit earlier each evening, I think I cherish those walks—both with company and without—even more. I know that before too long I'll be blowing into gloved hands and resenting the time I have to walk into a bitter breeze. So I had better enjoy the trees while they still have leaves and be happy that I'm striding along minus my barn coat and flannel-lined jeans, at least for a few weeks more.

In the past two or three days, it's not been so much what I've seen on my walks, but rather what I've heard. I know that to many, a life in the country doesn't seem very exciting, and for those of you who enjoy living elsewhere, I agree with Thoreau when he said that it's our prerogative to walk to the beat of different drummers. I'm just partial, especially after a day at work, to not hearing a drummer at all.

One of the first things I noticed on my walk a few days ago was the squeak of my own shoes. I wear a pair of running shoes for walking, and they sing a bit, at least until I get them warmed up. They create a sort of rhythm for me as I work into a pace, and after a while I don't notice them at all. I imagine I'll be wearing my mail-ordered waterproof hikers before long.

There's an atonal symphony of crickets playing in the weedy ditches along my route; some of the orchestra's sections are made up of other insects that I can't see, but that somehow know their days are numbered and want to spend those last few weeks alive making themselves known. Their music mingles with that of a chattering killdeer, worried that I may get too close to a nest long empty by this time of year.

There's more to hear than just the usual yapping dogs and passing cars; the wind blows across the bill of my cap and whistles past my ears, a confused rooster crows good morning despite it being nearly 6 in the evening, and a few sheep in need of haircuts bleat at no one in particular. They usually just ignore me as I waltz past their woven wire home anyway.

I walk into a cool dip in the road, a place where the sun creeps but a few minutes a day. We have learned to take care there because of limited walking space, so we often cross the road to find a place to get off to the side away from motorists who come over a rise not expecting to find us there. In that quiet spot, I've gotten into the habit of kicking shot put-sized hedge apples into the middle of the road to watch them curve back to my path a few feet farther along. There are remnants of the things on the road smashed by passing cars, and on one breezy day I was bombed by them as they fell out of the trees with a thud.

My wife and I always walk to a point where we know we can go no farther unless we want to be out after dark; it is a place where three pine trees sit alone alongside the road, and we often can smell them and hear the wind whistling through their needles as we make our turn and head for home. We wave at the cars that come up behind us without really looking back at who we're waving to; we often get a honk or hello from an open window.

With my back to the sun, I've heard the Canada geese as they honk their way off a pair of ponds a quarter mile apart. Between the two, there are several fields of soybeans, now turned to a drab gray from their earlier copper, and in the wind I hear them scraping together as if someone there is scratching his whiskered chin. In a week or two, the combines will have done their duty, and tractors will have pulled chisel-plows through the dark soil leaving the horizon open.

Further along, I hear the sandpaper rattle of dried corn leaves, the stalks so tall that I can't see the shape of the landscape on which they're grown until they, too, fall to the scythe of a combine. The sound of those leaves dancing in the wind is one of the loneliest sounds I think I've ever heard, one that suggests the corn itself knows its life has run its course.

Before I get home, I hear some unidentified flying object buzz past my ear and alight on a lone stalk of goldenrod; I think it's a grasshopper. It draws my attention to a sassafras tree ablaze in color and to a splendid chain of poison ivy that has turned to a bright red as it climbs its way up the side of a black gum tree that is itself turning a deep crimson. Near it, the road is splotched with the black oil of walnuts that have been hulled by passing cars. I often hear them smack the ground, not unlike the sound baseballs make as I listen to games on the radio on hot summer nights.

I kick a few of those walnuts along the asphalt like a kid kicking a can out of boredom, but I'm not bored at what I'm doing. I've often wondered why I've become so addicted to noise in my life; it seems to be the American way now. We play our televisions at dinner time, wear our headphones to put off listening to what is in our heads, talk just to have something to say. We ride when we can walk, sit when we can stand, go somewhere when we can just stay home. We're restless, but tired.

I may not really go anywhere on my walks; perhaps they're just hikes to no place in particular. But, ironically, the time on my feet keeps me grounded, keeps me listening for the sounds of the real world.

The 'Cat of the Baskervilles'
October 31, 2005

I've done more than my share of stupid things over the years, but perhaps the dumbest on my ledger in the past few weeks has to involve where I found myself a few Saturday nights ago.

My daughter's cat, George, went missing—he's usually on someone's lap sawing 'em off by early evening—and despite our earnest cat calls off our back deck and along our wood line, he was a no-show by 10:30. My little girl may not be very little anymore, but she has always been an animal lover, one whose devotion to alleviating pain and suffering in critters has often crossed the border between caring and craziness.

After coming to the understanding that she'd go into the wilds by herself if necessary, I joined her, lantern and flashlights in hand, crashing our way through the moonlit woods, calling out George's name as we worked our way down the steep hillsides, smacking ourselves in the face with branches and briars along the way. Occasionally, we'd stop and call for the cat, and sure enough, more than a quarter of a mile from our back step, we heard him.

I could tell that George wasn't moving and that he

was desperate, so we kept walking, and walking, over our back fence, across an abandoned railroad line, into what environmentalists might euphemistically call wetlands, but what most folks simply call a swamp. And, there was George. He was treed in a huge cottonwood, atop his own private island in the middle of a green, stagnant pool of rather ominous looking water. Picture naturalists searching for the ivory-billed woodpecker or Marlon Perkins going after crocs for "Wild Kingdom;" that's a fairly realistic picture of what George had gotten us into.

I've stated in an earlier story about our cats that George is a dim bulb. He was not going to come down from the tree had I installed an Otis elevator for him. My daughter and I stood together on a rotten log that was the closest thing to the base of George's repository (about 25 feet away) as we could get and soothingly tried to talk him down like a movie-actor air traffic controller tries to help a heroic insurance salesman land a passenger liner. It didn't happen.

Trying to convince my daughter to leave George where he was for the night was just as tough. She may have a college degree, have extraordinary common sense, and generally be an intelligent gal, but she was more than willing to stay in the woods all night if necessary. I wasn't.

Half an hour later, we had made our way up the hills to the house, put on grungier clothes and rubber boots, grabbed my battered extension ladder, argued a time or two, and were back once again below George's new-found penthouse apartment. I won't lie: It took a little mustered courage for me to take a step off that log into the fetid green muck that I hoped would not suddenly deepen before I reached the tree.

It's important to inject here that although I'm not paranoid about encounters with snakes, I don't encourage them either. I wasn't particularly interested in meeting anything else that might be lurking below the black surface. I don't mind telling you, we were in a pretty creepy place; the moon was nearly full, our breath puffed in the cold air, the coyotes were howling across the soybean fields, and something unknown was making a rather supernatural sound not far from the glow of our lantern light. The whole scene had a "Hound of the Baskervilles" feel to it, and I was no Basil Rathbone.

The ladder I own was my grandfather's; it's heavy and awkward and just creaky enough to make me feel uncomfortable on it. I extended it as far as it would go, stepped off into the slime, made my way to the cottonwood, and climbed as high as I could, still a good 10 feet shy of George's spot.

After a half hour of hoping he would crawl down to me and let me do the rest, it was obvious that George wasn't budging. Despite my son joining the rescue party, and then trying a vain attempt to extend an aluminum stepladder he brought down for me with one hand as I stood at the top of the other ladder, we eventually had to leave George alone for a long, cold, sleepless night. I can't tell you how tired I was by the time I left my grubby clothes in the garage to step into the house with a running nose and freezing hands.

By 7 the next morning, my daughter returned from the woods to announce that George was exactly where we left him the night before. My son said that a buddy of ours had an even longer extension ladder than ours, so we took off to get it. I can't explain it, but we were all optimistic that we'd get the cat out of the tree.

Within an hour, we did extract George from his rough-barked hell. I was able to climb to within six or seven feet of him, stand on my tiptoes, balance myself with one hand and reach up to palm his head with the other. I don't think he's left our backyard since I placed him in my daughter's arms, so maybe he's not as stupid as we thought. How he got in the tree or what chased him there will have to remain a mystery.

I tell you this story not because I'm planning to write a how-to guide on distressed pet recovery or am secretly yearning for some award from the American Society for the Prevention of Cruelty to Animals, either. It's to suggest that we'll go to great lengths to help our kids, to keep them from hurting. I don't think that parents should always pull their kids out of ruts; everyone needs a little failure in their lives, a little disappointment. But, they don't necessarily need it at the expense of a cat who managed to wander a bit too far from the safe haven of his home. My parents sacrificed for me, although I can't recall any pets they pulled out of trees in the process. I know they both worked hard and went without so I didn't have to.

You know, I've heard a few parents say they'd walk through fire for their kids. I don't know about that, but I'd walk through a swamp any day for mine.

Sometimes you don't see the forest for the trees
May 1, 2006

My wife and I own a few acres of woods; not much really but a shallow mine pond, a few groves of locust trees and some hills and hollows that hide from the sun most of the day. But they're ours to tramp in the spring when the Jack-in-the-Pulpits come out to show us their dappled arms and in the fall when the sugar maples turn yellow and drop their leafy blankets.

I grew up near the woods, spent much of my young life in the gently rolling land between my house and the sandy fields that bordered it. It was a pretty place, spotted with tulip poplars and shallow washes that hid gray mushrooms among delicate ferns and the musty scent of rotting wood.

My parents, and especially my dad's dad, loved the woods. As far back as I can remember, I can recall walking those woods with my mom, a packed lunch and a jug of water socked away next to a favorite sycamore tree, a plastic bread sack stuffed in the back pocket of my patched blue jeans, and a walking stick in my hand that I used to pick through leaves, whack branches, and out-duel imaginary foes if need be.

Most of us drive past the woods on our way home or

to shopping or restaurants; I am guilty of that myself. I guess I didn't have any place particular to go when I was a kid, but I was richer for spending a lot of my time in the woods.

Now, it seems as though folks often buy property to make their investment back in pulpwood or upturned property values, but it seems to me that we often don't see the forest for the trees. My wife and I bought our property knowing it had already been mined out and logged out years ago, that it's a tangled maze of wild roses and hedgeapple trees. But it's okay with us to know that the deer and the cottontails and red-shouldered hawks have the run of our place. It was theirs before it was ours anyway.

I don't get away from my schedule and deskwork enough to walk our woods like I should. Like just about every other Hoosier, I hunt mushrooms in the spring, and so I make an effort to pencil in an occasional evening away from my mowers and ungraded papers or ball games to wander around and poke my nose into the kinds of places I once thought were a young explorer's paradise. I still have an attraction for water-tumbled gravel and sassafras leaves and skipping thin stones across a pond.

It's odd, but I'll pick through a quarter of an acre of hillside on my hands and knees and forget that I even have on a watch for an hour at a time as I search for spongy yellow treasures, yet I have never acquired a taste for mushrooms. My wife will fry them up after giving them a tumble in flour and butter and salt, but despite the lure of the crunch and the calories, I still prefer searching for mushrooms to eating them, a deal my family finds agreeable.

When I was a kid and lived in northern Vigo County, I used to find so many mushrooms that I gave them away to my relatives and friends at church. Even then I had critics who thought that I had spent too much time in the sun and had lost my mind. But now, whether it is global warming or pollution or ground that's been too often fenced and stocked with cattle, my Parke County clay doesn't yield mushrooms like the sandy soil of my boyhood home. But I also have to say that what's on my mind is as much at fault as what's in the dirt. Time has become money, and while I walk the woods I often let the paperwork and shaggy grass that await me in the back of my mind ruin the quiet time I have sought.

There is something about the woods in the spring that gives me hope. Although I know there are a million life-and-death struggles going on under my feet as I tromp about—not unlike those in the Middle East or those of fractured families and the drug abuse at our doorsteps—I feel that much of that hate and pain and desperation would somehow be resolved by the simple pleasure of watching the shimmering reflection of a brilliant white dogwood on quiet water. I know that's naïve, but I can't help myself, and on a day when the sky is blue and the sun is warm on my back, all is right with an imperfect world.

Years ago, I held hands with my young family and

walked up a steep hill to the North Carolina home of Carl Sandburg, known mostly as an Illinois boy poet, but a gardener and woodland walker near Asheville as an older man. On a sign near a pond at the base of the hill an inscription from Sandburg's pen read: "I may keep this boyheart of mine. I am an idealist. I don't know where I am going, but I am on my way."

I had that passage in mind last week as I high-stepped my way through the brush of my own woods, walking across land that my family owns but has not yet made our own by knowing it well. As I did, and as I walked through outcroppings of moss-covered stone that had been worn by centuries in the sun and snow, past the delicate lavender stands of Sweet William and the broad leaves and yellow-white flowers of Mayapples, I was, just for a little while, a boy, back at home in my woods, in a place that I can't go to anymore since it was sold off years ago.

Like Sandburg, I may not know where I'm going, but I hope that I keep my boyheart too.

Lighthouse a reminder to leave footprints on the sands of time
July 10, 2006

As I sit at my desk to write this piece, the heat of an Indiana July has come in on the tide of a southwest wind. Just a few days ago, I sat in the cooler breeze of another place and watched spikes of marram grass bend as if pushed over by an invisible hand.

Since our children have grown, their busier lives have kept us from loading up the family car for long summer vacations as we used to do when they occupied themselves in our backseat with mile after mile of spotting license plates, staring contests, and snacking on the Cheerios that my wife carried in a bag for them. A few years ago we discovered, quite by accident, the Lake Michigan shoreline and its blue-green waters and shifting sand dunes. This year, we returned to discover even more.

My wife and I have always loved lighthouses. One of those longer trips years ago was to Nags Head, North Carolina, where the ages-old lighthouses there are quaint reminders of the perils of the Atlantic both then and now. On one of my office walls is a framed print I brought home from that trip. Its watercolors depict six lighthouses along the Carolina coast with names like Bodie Island Light and Cape Fear Light, all built in the 19th century.

A number of travel guides reminded me that Lake Michigan has been no less fierce a place than the shoals and shallows of the Carolinas' waters. There are 124 lighthouses scattered along the 3,200 miles of Lake Michigan's coastline, and the deep cold waters of that deceivingly beautiful graveyard hold the sunken remains of nearly 10,000 ships.

We have never been an amusement park kind of family, and this year was no exception. We drove north well along Michigan's coastline to stay near Silver Lake, which, like its vastly larger neighbor, was carved out of the sand and gravel of the region by the last of the great glaciers. Just a mile from where we slept and ate and hiked the massive dunes sits a lighthouse called Little Sable Point, the tallest lighthouse on Lake Michigan. It was built 132 years ago.

All that remains of Little Sable Point today is the tower itself. The house that once stood with it was razed years ago, as were the landing docks originally used to bring in the bricks and other building materials to construct the place. Restored in 1997, all that sits with the lighthouse along that stretch of beach is a massive cottonwood tree, a pile of huge limestone chunks, and thin stands of native sea rockets, beach peas, and black willows.

On the day we spent looking things over there, only a handful of people were on the beaches with us, and few were brave enough to test the cool water with more than an ankle-deep wade in the shallows. The sun was warm on our faces, but a steady and stiff west wind that would blow thunderstorms across the lake a day later kept us hoping that what clouds were in the sky wouldn't spend much time with us. We explored the dunes and watched the horizon as it changed in the light, but mostly we just sat and listened to the lapping water and the thoughts in our own heads.

It's odd, perhaps a bit crazy, but as I stretched out, an elbow dug into a wind-swept bank of sand, I didn't just see the lighthouse as it was that day, but also how it must have appeared on a night a century ago. As the light's keeper worked to provide his beacon, I could almost hear the foghorn of an ore ship lost off the point, a lonely plea for help through a cold, gray mist.

We stayed late into the day knowing that we'd not be back to Little Sable Point, perhaps ever. Each of us grew drowsy and lazy, and each in turn slept a little while too. My son napped a little more seriously than the rest of us, lying on his belly with his face resting on his arms for three-quarters of an hour, sprawled on the sand like a shipwreck survivor.

By the time the sun was creeping closer to the horizon, our legs a little stiff and our stomachs a lot empty, we walked past the lighthouse and up a sandy trail to our car. I tagged along last like a kid who just couldn't bear to leave a particularly fun day behind. I suppose that was the main reason we took the time to stop to see yet another old lighthouse near Holland as we made our way south and home a day later.

In a poem that he wrote as an old man, Henry Longfellow lamented about the tide rising and falling and the fact that it erases our solitary trip across the beach—speaking metaphorically of the one pass we make in life and that most recollections of us are eventually washed away. The poem may be a solemn reminder of our mortality, but I'd rather think of other lines in another poem that he wrote when he was younger. In it, he encouraged us to "leave our footprints on the sands of time," that we can be an inspiration for our "shipwrecked and forlorn" brothers—not unlike the lighthouse we explored at

Little Sable Point.

Each of us has fragments of memories of days long past that for some reason or another stay with us to the grave. For a man who has lived his whole life near the woods and creeks and straight endless fields of corn rows and soybeans, I treasure the time I've spent near the sea and along the Great Lakes with my family.

Our footprints already have been washed away, but not our memories of that place.

A peaceful walk through Terre Haute's history August 21, 2006

Regardless of my love for history, I know the subject is often perceived as being a little dry. But the kind of history that Roxe Anne Kesner teaches, despite the fact that she does most of it while walking among one of the quietest crowds in town, is far from dull.

Kesner is officially called the clerk of Terre Haute's City Cemetery Department, but I like to think of her as a teacher. Despite her title—she is primarily the office manager at Highland Lawn Cemetery, handling payrolls, accounts payable and receivable, burials, records, and genealogical research— she simply says, "I am a public servant, and I feel that it is important to give people the kind of service that I'd appreciate myself."

One of those services, and the one that Kesner loves above all others, is taking those who are interested on guided tours of Highland Lawn, the second largest cemetery in Indiana with its 139 acres of rolling hills, majestic bell tower, and Romanesque chapel.

The cemetery opened in 1884, primarily because the other city-owned burial ground, Woodlawn, was nearing capacity after the city relocated its first cemetery (located at 6th and Ohio) and the Indian Orchard Cemetery on 1st Street. It is an excellent example of late 19th century Romantic (Victorian) landscape design and was placed on the National Register and the State Registry of Historic Places in 1991.

Kesner was born in Lebanon, Indiana, grew up in Cincinnati, and graduated from Western Boone High School before coming to Indiana State. Despite working in banking for many years, she always had an interest in teaching history, a passion fostered by encouraging parents.

Married to her childhood sweetheart, and the mother of two college-aged children, Kesner took on her job quite by accident in 1994. On the day that she quit her job in banking 11 years ago, she visited her husband, Phil, who works for the city in planning and redevelopment. Mayor Pete Chalos, who heard from Phil about her job status, took her into his office and offered her the job that she's worked at ever since.

How did the office manager become a tour guide? "When I began working here, Rita Kendall was the superintendent," Kesner says. "One day, she drove me through Highland Lawn and began to tell me about the people buried here. She had a love for the entire place and it reflected in her voice. She said she had started doing tours and there was a tour coming up later that week, and I would be doing it... I was shocked, but the tour came and went, and I've done too many to count since then."

The list of notables in Highland Lawn is long and impressive. It is the repository of John Heinl, master of the legendary Stiffy Green, the tomb of the eccentric Martin Sheets, who had a telephone installed in his mausoleum, and the world-famous poet Max Ehrmann. Local businessman Chauncey Rose is buried there, as is five-time socialist presidential candidate Eugene Debs, and Dr. Frank Wiedemann, who developed the first x-ray machine to be used in the United States. The cemetery's registry is a virtual "Who's Who" of recognizable local names from Vern McMillan, Ralph and Ruth Tirey, Demas Deming, William Rea, and Chapman Root.

William Wash Williams, the man who, as a reporter for the New York Sunday World, completed his assignment to find one William Sydney Porter, otherwise known to the world as "O. Henry" is also at Highland Lawn; Daniel Voorhees, the three-time United States senator is there, too, as are Swopes and Tuckers, McLeans and Wileys, Dobbses and Blumbergs. Claude Herbert, a young department store Santa Claus, is buried at Highland; he died saving women and children in an enormous downtown Terre Haute fire in 1898.

With too many stories to tell in a two or three-hour

tour, Kesner still enjoys one story more than all the rest. "My favorite person is Ellen Church Marshall," Kesner says as her eyes light up.

Marshall began her career as a nurse after graduating from the University of Minnesota, then served our country in the U.S. Army Nurse Corps from 1942 to 1946, traveling through Africa, Europe, and the United States. She served 20 months evacuating wounded soldiers from the front lines, and she was the first woman to receive the Air Medal, the EAME Campaign Medal with seven bronze service stars, the American Theater Campaign Medal, and the Victory Medal. She first proposed the concept of the airline stewardess to the predecessor of United Airlines, and became a chief stewardess herself. She came to Terre Haute in 1951 as Director of Nurses at the School of Nursing at Union Hospital, then became the administrator to the hospital.

"What a wonder woman," Kesner says. "She was a heroine to many. But, I also love telling the story of Stiffy Green, and that's the one most people want to hear."

A natural storyteller, Kesner believes we all like to hear stories, perhaps because "everyone has a story to tell," she says. "Highland Lawn is a perfect place to learn the rich history of this city and county. I love the grounds, the architecture, the massive stones, and the stories they tell on their own. It makes you want to go back to a time long ago when Terre Haute was a bustling city."

Does Kesner plan to become part of the folklore of Highland Lawn herself, perhaps be a stop on someone else's walking tour someday?

"I don't own graves here yet," she says, "But someday, when I am buried here, maybe one of the students who've been through here with me will walk by and say, 'That lady told me so much about the history of this great city.' Then, maybe they'll pass on some of the stories to their children."

Kesner says she regrets never getting a college degree in history, but adds, "This is the one place I can still teach and make an impact on one or two lives."

I'd say it's been more than that.

Reflecting on my own trip to bountiful
November 22, 2006

One of my favorite treasures sits on a shined oak desktop next to the smiling faces of old photographs, an odd assortment of collected rocks and beach-combed shells, and the clipped cords of a championship basketball net. It's a first edition copy of Ernie Pyle's "Home Country," a book that left its handprint on me after I read the very first line Pyle wrote in its very first chapter called Home in Indiana. In just those few words, Pyle suggests something that I have come to feel about living in this place I call home.

Pyle wrote, "I don't know whether you know that long, sad wind that blows so steadily across thousands of miles of Midwest flatlands in the summertime. If you don't, it will be hard for you to understand the feeling I have about it. Even if you do know it, you may not understand."

I think I do know what Pyle felt, and I felt it most recently on a cool but sunny Saturday afternoon as I drove my son and wife north up old State Road 13 and away from the state capital. Although he's done well in the classroom in his first year in college, my boy still feels the tugs of football and small school friendship, so we've spent our fall weekends rolling over the Indiana countryside to look at campuses on which he may yet be walking next year. Our destination that day was North Manchester, a college town with maple-lined streets and the scent of academic charm in its air. But on that day, it was the barns and farms and the last leaf color of the dying fall that held my attention most.

My writing here is no travelogue like Pyle's, nothing as good as what Charles Kuralt or Bill Bryson have penned, just my observations of what we saw as we drove the smooth two-lane pavement through some of that wind-blown farmland Pyle so fondly remembered.

The trip to North Manchester took me away from the biggest city in the state through some of its smallest, but it didn't take much time nor very many miles north of Indianapolis to see something of which Pyle saw very little of in his day. When Pyle was alive, the concept of the suburb was a relatively new thing; people either lived in the city or lived in or near small towns. A lot of folks considered themselves lucky to have a neighbor down the road a half mile or so.

I know that progress must be made and money invested, that tearing down and building up are uniquely human traits that have manifested themselves for centuries, but the wholesale destruction of farmland and woods that we saw that day made me wonder whether we can afford to lose much more to the jaws of dozers and graders and chainsaws, particularly so our quick drives to gas up the car or pick up a prescription will be cut by a few minutes. That is exactly what I was pondering as we finally drove past the outskirts of the urban sprawl and into the yet unharvested cornfields that rattled in the dry breezes that blew across them from the west.

Although I had driven that road at least once before on some weekend adventure, I hadn't remembered where Lapel, Fishersburg, or Perkinsville were until that day. We drove near Aroma and smelled nothing unusual, and we idled through downtown Elwood, the hometown of 1940 presidential hopeful Wendell Wilkie.

I remembered seeing Wilkie in a black-and-white history book photograph, standing in the back of a convertible, wild-eyed, his arms outstretched, the dust of Main Street rolling up behind him. He was back in Elwood for a triumphant return to his Hoosier roots, just a few months before FDR crushed him in the election. I knew that he had become a Wall Street lawyer who had left Indiana years before, but I wondered if he, too, felt the familiarity of the wind Pyle spoke of that day.

We leisurely drove through Leisure and Point Isabel, and, I suppose we felt like most other passers-by as we made our way through Normal. As we headed into Swayzee I remembered that the now defunct high school teams there were proudly called the Speed Kings, but as in the case of too many tiny burgs like that town, the only proud bearer of that once-revered nickname was a tiny restaurant along the highway whose reference to the name applied to the quickness of its pizza delivery.

Through Mier, past Somerset and Mount Vernon, we drove and gabbed and laughed our way to Wabash, which, in the spring of 1880, became the first "electrically lighted city in the world." I was just as impressed to see a few hills as we crossed the banks of the Wabash before we came to the town, a bit of rare geography in those parts. I hardly had to take my foot off the accelerator as we cruised through Speicherville and Urbana on our last leg to North Manchester.

When we turned around and headed home a few hours later, all that stood in our way was a quick bite to eat, a fast fill-up, and the repetitive drone of the road; much of our conversation had died down as we just watched the sun set in scarlets and pinks off our right shoulders.

I contemplated a side trip to the Mississinewa battleground, but I was more tired than interested by then. I even considered exploring State Road 18, a skinny ribbon of blacktop that would take us west and back home through Lafayette. After all, I'd never been to Converse or Wawpecong, Bennett's Switch or Young America. But they'd have to wait for another day.

Before going on to tell a story about his childhood, Pyle wrote this in that opening chapter: "Maybe it's a bad job, my trying to make you see something that only I can ever feel."

I know exactly what he meant.

'Roughing it' has taken on a different meaning December 18, 2006

A relatively rare December thunderstorm swept through my neck of the woods last Tuesday night. At the first hint of lightning, I hurried to unplug our computer—the victim of a strike before—then stood looking out our front door as the wind began to paste fat raindrops against the glass. I could see our leafless trees bending a little in the garish glare of craggy flashes of white. Then, our lights flickered, and then dimmed just enough to cast the house in a sepia-toned half-light.

I whisked through the house, clicking off Christmas lights and living room lamps, hoping that what little juice we were receiving was going to be just enough to keep our refrigerator purring and our water pump pumping. Within minutes, the lights simply evaporated; the house instantly dark and silent. It was a little after eight, and an already wet, dreary day looked bright by comparison to our pitch black house that almost immediately began to cool.

The crews who work our power lines and substations are a hearty bunch, so I didn't bother to call anyone about our troubles. We've had outages before, and it usually takes less than an hour before we see hard-hatted men in bucket trucks cruising the roads in search of the problem. I've never felt it necessary to invest in a generator; flashlights and candles, coal oil lamps and a fireplace have always done the trick.

My son was studying at the kitchen table for a final test in one of his college courses when the power went off; my wife sat across from him sorting through coupons and Christmas lists. I grabbed an old glass lamp that had been my grandmother's off a book case in my office, struck a single match to its wick, turned it just high enough to avoid a plume of black smoke, and walked away to let them share the light, which they did, unexpectedly, for a good while.

Even our cat knew something was up. Arthur knows the sound of our humidifier, likes to sleep under the lights of our Christmas tree, often curls himself into a ball in an old beanbag chair in our living room to spend his evening in front of the television. But that night, he came to the kitchen for companionship.

I had graded my papers for the evening, had already showered and laid out my clothes for the next day of school too, so I stumbled my way into our bedroom and found a clip-on book light that I've been known to use on the sly when sleep becomes a stranger to me. I shoved the light into a book I've been trying to read for a while now, then let it show me the way to our family room where I plopped down in a chair to read until the lights came back on.

I'm sure that a number of people that night—families used to televisions blaring in every room, to dishwashers humming, stereos playing, and lights just the flip of a switch away—considered themselves to be roughing it in a way. Americans have become so used to convenience, to comfort, to warmth and sound and water and entertainment, whenever we want them, that to be without them, even for a few minutes, must feel strange and unsettling. At first, it seemed that way for me too.

But as I sat in the chair, my feet propped up, the light doing little to show me much past the page I was reading, I came to enjoy the darkness and the quiet and the cool. Besides the ringing that often plagues my ears, I could hear the light tapping of rainwater as it dropped from the gutters through the corner downspouts, the tap of it reminding me of a coded but consistent message. I heard the house itself creak as it slowly cooled, like a car clicking in the drive after a long trip. I could hear the wind skittering leaves along the concrete walk outside our door too.

I've never lived without the convenience of electricity. Although I grew up in a house where air conditioning was a foreign concept, that was partially heated by a wood-burning stove, that had a party-line telephone with a dial, and that had a small, single bathroom that often left at least one of us hopping on one foot outside its door, I've never known what it was like to turn on a faucet and not get hot water, to read by oil lamp light, to huddle around a fireplace as my sole source of heat.

My dad used to tell me how it was to live during the Great Depression, powerless in more ways than one. Before the rural cooperatives brought current out to the farms on the county line in the mid-40s, he read by the glow of lamplight on many winter nights, his family and friends slept out on their front porches, or in the yard, in the summer to beat the heat of the house, and a trip to the privy late at night in any season was always inconvenient, sometimes traumatic, with its black snakes, spider webs, and cold toilet seats.

On this past Thanksgiving night, I sat with one of my brothers-in-law, a nephew, and my father-in-law, Gib, in a dark farmhouse dining room, lit only by a fireplace that Nick, the nephew, stokes to perfection whenever the family gets together. Cloistered from the noise of a gabbing group, we talked a little bit of politics, a little bit of religion, and did a little reminiscing. When the topic got around to the Depression years and entertainment, Nick asked his grandpa what he did at night when there was no power, no television, no CD players. "We went to bed early," Gib said in his usual monosyllabic deadpan.

After a solid hour of darkness in my chair, my eyes grew heavy; I figured the book I was reading was still not going to get finished anytime soon. I dragged my weary bones through the kitchen, past my wife and son as they sat in the glow of the lamp, and following Gib's advice, plopped into bed.

I tossed an extra blanket over my feet, since the house was cooler yet, said my goodnights, and quickly fell asleep in a silent house. For an hour more the only sound within hearing distance was the rain running in the gutters outside our windows, perhaps that of my own snoring. I awoke only when the power came back on. With it came the voices of a television in another room; the reds and greens of Christmas lights crawling under my bedroom door, and I felt the heat from my furnace warming the room.

Roughing it was over.

Window view on a winter's day just right
January 4, 2007

I kept an eye trained out my window to the windy ice box of my front yard as I wrote this story. A blue-white nuthatch tap danced his way head-first down one of my silver maple trees to a wooden bird feeder that is little more than a pressure-treated serving tray. I poured a mound of seeds and cracked corn into the tray a while earlier, hoping that my feathered friends hadn't pecked it completely clean while I was away at work, but they had.

No sooner had I turned my back on the fill-up than the birds came to it as if I'd rung their dinner bell, not unlike our fat cat, Arthur, who expels by far the most energy of his sloth-like day trotting to his bowl as soon as he hears it rattled or filled. We have gotten into the cruel habit these days of brushing up against his dish just to help him get a little aerobic exercise by hopping on and off our sofa.

My wife and I have always fed the birds. We have felt it our duty to help them make it through the winter, knowing full well that the handful of faithful followers we feed is nothing when compared to the countless numbers of beaked cousins and friends who somehow missed the gravy train. Life must be harder for them as they flit from branch to briar looking for that solitary and withered berry, that scrap or morsel left by others who are too full to have taken it all.

Years ago, I had a half-dozen feeders going in our back yard. I eventually grew tired of fighting the raccoons and the squirrels that alternated between brazen daylight raiding parties and stealthy nighttime missions for the leftover seed. Then there were our own cats, who soon discovered that if they were just patient enough, some poor preoccupied finch or cardinal would concentrate on his meal more than on self-preservation.

Now, we keep just one feeder going, leaving it only full enough to satisfy our friends and frustrate their enemies. The cats seem to stay occupied searching for victims in the back yard now, or are so hooked on tuna-flavored cat food that a mouth full of feathers and feet holds little appeal to them anymore.

My mom fed the birds with a passion. I began to fill her feeders when I was a kid, often tossing in the occasional ear of corn I had picked up from gleaning the fields next to our house. She would stand at our kitchen window for hours to watch the birds peck away at the potato peels or table scraps that she had tossed into the fence row. I found her every once in a while sitting at our kitchen table, a bird book and a cup of coffee for companions.

For the most part, our feeder is visited by a cast of regulars. Like buddies who bend elbows at the bar, they alternate between gracious turn-taking and brawling over some coveted seat. Our clientele is mostly cardinals and sparrows, titmice and sparrows, blue jays and red-bellied woodpeckers, the latter who rule the roost if they want to.

I think of all our visitors I find female cardinals the prettiest. Unlike their mates, they have little flashiness to them, but their browns and nearly-oranges are subtle and elegant. The jays seem to me to be bullies; they rarely share among themselves, let alone with the other birds. They usually hover somewhere on the perimeter or feed on the ground to pick up what has been dropped in the feeding frenzy. The woodpeckers wield their beaks like policeman batons, and even the jays pay attention to their orders.

I was in a grain store a few years ago buying a bag of birdseed. As I neared the cash register, an older man in brown overalls told me that he thought it was silly to feed the birds, that people like me were making wild things weaker by leaving them corn and salt and suet, an opinion that couldn't have made the store's proprietor very happy. The man said that our hobby was making animals more dependent on man; he wasn't kidding.

If our front yard birds are dependent upon us for their meals, so be it. We rely on them too. Their flashes of blue and red and brown make the winter whites and grays, the bare branches and frozen ground, more bearable for us. Besides, I walked out to the barn this evening, wrapped in a flannel-lined coat, my hands covered with gloves, a scarf wrapped around my neck, and a hood pulled over my head. I still shivered and hurried to get my chores done and back into my warm house. It's moments like those that remind me that the birds I'm "helping" are tougher than I am anyway; they can get along without me just fine if they have to.

My wife often stands at the kitchen window to watch the feeder, and I sit at my writing desk, a cup of coffee and a book nearby. Our view is just right.

Perfectionism, bad back are a pain in the grass May 21, 2007

This story may sound like one of those middle-aged complaints we're all familiar with. I simply got out of bed one morning two weeks ago, felt a little tug in my lower back, and am now a serious candidate for traction.

You'd think that I would be worried about fixing my back, but right now I'm only concerned about dealing with the pain coursing through it—an intensely annoying mixture of small atomic explosions radiating down my left leg and a continually sharp punch delivered just below my kidneys by an angry United States Marine.

I have managed to crawl out of bed and get to work; I have cut a few corners by staying seated behind my desk a little more; I have tried to do as much stretching as I can between doctor's visits, injections, and heading to the pharmacy. Despite fighting the good fight, nothing has worked yet.

But sadly, the thing that is most on my mind is getting my yard work done. My grass needs cut, my trees trimmed, and my hedges clipped. I know, my concern is a bit irrational.

It's probably my mom that I have to blame for my intense dislike for things being out of order, unkempt, or in disrepair, and it is my family that suffers the most for that quirk in my nature. Mom may have never used the exact words, but I'm positive that she believed that "everything has a place, and there's a place for everything," and I cannot give it recess from my mind.

I can still remember an instance years ago when I used to stick around after school just to drive my boy home from football practice—kind of a nice dependency he had on me then since it gave us time to decompress and talk for a few minutes about what had transpired each day. Anyway, it was hot and moist and August, and I was hurrying home. He wanted to know why I was in such a rush.

"I have some grass to cut behind the house tonight,

and I want to get it done before supper," I said.

"Why mow it tonight?" he asked. "No one sees that spot anyway."

"I see it," I said, and he was soon resigned to the fact that I was going to mow that little plot of crabgrass along the woods, and I was going to do it regardless of the fact that I was already hot and tired, and the day was a humid oven. I wanted it done. After all, I had a fencerow that needed trimmed back, and that was the next night's project.

I think he considered himself lucky that I let him concentrate on football practice and homework, instead of asking for his help. Many of my students at school feel I ask too much of them, that I set expectations an inch or two higher than they can jump. I know my editors probably find it irritating that I'll re-send corrected copy to them because I feel I've misplaced a comma or I've re-worked a particularly clumsy passage; I should learn to be more trusting that my errors will be caught and fixed. My neighbor must be tired of hearing my gas trimmer or push mower in the evenings, too, wondering how often I need to tidy up, and how neatly I have to keep the grass.

There's a poem I've read by Robert Frost about a man who stumbles across a cord of neatly stacked wood while he's wandering through a forest tract. The poet contemplated that few people, if any, would know of the hours of work the unknown and unseen laborer had spent there, and that the wood, already sitting for a year or two, might never be used. Frost felt that perhaps it was work done just for the sake of working.

I often think of that poem when I'm in some remote corner of my property, or while I'm painting the back of my barn, or pulling pesky weeds from a hillside that no one sees but me. No one outside of my family knows what I've truly done, the hours I've spent in toil, the sweat I've invested. But, I've never really done it for anyone else; it's been a selfish venture, I guess.

Right now, as I face a little more down time than I'd like, and a lot more pain than I care to deal with, too, I am going to have to rely on my son to help me do many of the chores around my place that I like to usually take care of myself out of a matter of foolish pride.

I know he's up to the job because he's already had a life in which he knows he's supposed to work. He's mastered hay baling, fence-post pulling, and rock spreading. When he's not in school or working his day job, he's mowing his grandpa's yard or washing his truck or hitting the weight room. And, come to think of it, he's a bit of a perfectionist, as well, a guy who keeps his lines straight and even. I think we'll be okay.

Now, does anybody have an aspirin the size of a baseball?

The good old days weren't always that great
July 17, 2007

Before you write or call to tell me that I should get over

the way it used to be years ago and warm up to a few modern conveniences, please, by all means, read on.

I happened to see an old Pepsi Cola sign in a restaurant a few weeks ago—a slightly rusted metal masterpiece depicting a cold bottle of the product, ever so slightly tipped with beads of condensation slowly dripping down its sides. I was enraptured, and as is often the case with such nostalgic things, I took a little side trip from reality to the days when I used to drink Pepsi out of my grandma's refrigerator after I'd finished mowing her yard.

Regardless of progress in packaging and marketing, there is no way that bottled soda pop is as good as it was 30 or 40 years ago. If anybody can reproduce the incredible sensation of whisking into Al Nagy's Texaco out on the County Line Road in the blast furnace heat of late July, of sticking my hand into the frigid waters of an aluminum-lined tub of ice near his west window and yanking out 12 ounces of glass-encased liquid gold called brown cream soda, well, I'd be happy to pay for the privilege.

In those days, I could guzzle Orange Crush and root beer, Grape Nehi and oh-so-delicious black cherry soda—out of real bottles, not paper-thin aluminum cans that are warm within minutes. Even more detestable are plastic bottles; they remind me of sipping tepid water out of a garden hose left in the sun. Ask anyone who can recall the days when they could drop a dime into a pop machine, open its slender, vertical door, and give his favorite drink a satisfying yank, and you'll bring back pleasant memories.

As if that ritual wasn't spiritual enough, we were able to—in our own individual style—pop the bottle's top using the machine's built-in opener. It was even a rite of passage for some aspiring he-men to try to open the bottles with their bare hands.

My point is this: There are some things that can't be improved upon: cold pop in glass bottles is one of them. Shopping for Christmas gifts in a real downtown district is another (extra points scored if lights are strung across the streets and it's snowing), and watching a movie in a real movie theater instead of a claustrophobic mall cubicle is another.

Going to a gas station isn't nearly as satisfying now. Most "service stations" today are mini-marts. You can buy a hot latte or lottery ticket or gallon of milk there, but most often you're going to pay 4 bits for a few pounds of compressed air so you can drive on down the road in search of somebody who can actually repair a tire.

I can remember a time when you heard the metallic clank of a bell as you pulled your car into a station. The owner/mechanic would put down his oily rags and hand tools to step outside and ask, "Fill 'er up?" While you hunted through your wallet for a few dollars, the gentleman would pop your hood, check your oil, clean your windshield, and plump your tires if they needed a breath of air. He did all of that when gas was 38 cents a gallon.

Before I really get going—I feel a series coming on

here—I have to mention a few things that are clearly better now, and the first has to be automobiles.

When I think of the first car I can remember my family having, I simply recall how hot and dusty it was. We owned a dull, gray-green Chevy coupe, and it had to have had the scratchiest seats ever made. It had no power steering or power brakes or carpeting or back windows that rolled all the way down. It seems as though it often needed the wheel bearings re-packed with grease, that its tires never lasted very long—you always shopped for them by how many "ply" they had—and it was as bulky and ugly as a Sherman tank.

I know that cars probably cost a larger percentage of our yearly wages now, but what a difference in comfort and performance. Cars now have memory seats, and we can listen to crystal-clear satellite radio and compact discs, and, of course, the truest testament to technology, air-conditioning, which has become standard equipment. I can now use my cruise control and defrost my rear window and change the speed on my windshield wipers and get 50,000 miles out of a set of tires. I wish I had taken a photo of my first car for a scrapbook, but I wouldn't trade my ride now for my first three cars.

Another thing we do better now, although dealing with insurance companies and paying exorbitant fees are a major pain included in the package, is doctoring and medicine. Sure, I have to visit my doctor at his office now, sometimes waiting a good while in the bargain to see him, when, in the old days if I was sick enough, Dr. Fell would actually drive over to our house wearing his typical white shirt and black pants and carrying his little black bag. He'd walk right into my bedroom with a stethoscope around his neck, brought most of his own medicine with him in little white boxes, and sometimes even gave me a shot, like the time I suffered from impetigo and lay blistered and feverish on our living room couch.

But I also know that my doctor now, Dr. Thomas Nicholas, has a lot of advanced testing at his disposal; he's well-read and well-educated, and he can give me a shot using a tiny needle that is a dream compared to the demonic, saber-like monsters that used to leave me screaming after my latest tetanus injection. Doc, and his partner, Daniel Dwyer, have stitched me up and X-rayed me and listened to me complain for nearly 30 years now. Just a few summers ago, Doc medicated me for hornet stings that as a child were poorly treated with a baking soda poultice; what a difference.

My doctor can order tests that Dr. Fell never lived to see developed, and I am convinced that had medicine been where it is today, my mom's dad would have lived past his 38th birthday to see his youngest grandson born, and that my dad's mom would not have died at 60 with an "inoperable" brain tumor. No, there's no comparison to make between medicine then and now, and I get shivers up my spine when I remember what a trip to a dentist was like 40 years ago.

I could go on, and perhaps will in another installment. Why, I haven't even written about televisions and tennis shoes, telephones and toys. Make no mistake about it, though, not everything from the good old days was that good.

Making one final cut in the field before fall
August 27, 2007

I stationed myself last weekend at the corner of a tiny garden plot that we keep near the north side of our barn, a spewing green garden hose in my hand giving my tomatoes a badly-needed gulp of water while the brown grass on which I stood crunched under my feet.

We can't give our potted plants enough water these days, but years ago, during a similar dry and dusty summer, my wife and I agreed that we wouldn't water our lawn just to keep it green. We'd wait on the master gardener himself to do that and save the water for more desperate needs.

Despite it being decidedly August and 95 degrees and as muggy as a barber's shaving towel, I couldn't help but sense some feeling for fall that day. The ivy that trellises up the trees along our wood line is growing red, and our yellow poplar is showing a hint of its namesake color as well. Our tiger lilies are nothing but shriveled yellow ghosts of themselves, and only the hostas we have planted in deep shade have avoided the anemia that their sunned counterparts have been fated by my poor planning.

Another sure sign that fall can't be very far off—a season I certainly welcome with open arms each year—

is that my friend, Joe Huxford, told me the other night that it was just about time to cut his hay for a third and final time. He's mowed and raked and baled it a fourth time as late as the waning days of September—even in early October in rare years that have had abundant warmth and moisture—but the brick oven bakery quality of this summer makes that unlikely.

Joe loves to bale hay, and he loves to do it much like his father and his grandfather used to. To this day I still see a little light in his eyes in the spring when he says he's going to get his old hay rake and bolt-busting baler ready for a season of hard labor. He may be a carpenter and a grandpa and a handyman, but everything else comes to a halt in his life when it's time to bale.

I've worked a little hay for Joe over the years, not for money, but to simply help repay him for some kindness or favor. He's had an easier time getting me to head to the fields with him when it's been straw to put up. Straw is kinder to my allergies and my back, but these days I'd just as soon know that I'm not taking worthy labor away from some deserving teenaged boy who needs the money for movies and gas and girls.

I started to bale hay, as most country kids did years ago, when I turned 12 or 13; I was six feet tall by then, and my uncle, who baled a few acres, thought that any boy my size should be making his own way in the world. No farmer baled hay into the Volkswagon-sized round bales as they do now; most still had his laborers walk alongside the wagon and pick up the bales as they fell from the baler, then tote them to a moving wagon for the stackers to nip and tuck them into place. Only when crews were short or farmers merciful did you work a wagon that was attached to the baler. That innovation enables the worker to pull the bales directly onto the wagon with a hook. If anyone has ever put up hay, he or she knows that handling bales fewer times is a good thing, as does Joe for he employs that method.

Working in the hay mount (often called the loft) is for the sturdiest of hay handlers. August heat, tin barn roofs, and chaff so thick that you blow it out of your nose for days makes one look for the final bale of every load, the bale a friend of mine used to call, "The one we've been looking for all day." It's not uncommon for hay mounts to reach 120 degrees on a hot summer day, and stepping out of one to meet even the hint of a faint breeze is like peering into an open refrigerator in your kitchen.

I used to bale for my father-in-law when he was still farming and had horses and cattle to feed. I remember that a neighbor of his used to bring his baler off the ridge to Gib's valley farm and get the hay on the ground for him. Being just the two of us, we would let his old tractor idle its way along as we worked the load together in a frenzied choreography of tossing bales and jumping on and off the wagon. Believe me, a two-man baling operation helps you sleep well at night.

Joe tells me that he has more trouble getting hay help these days; years ago kids were eager to have the money and the work and would ask him when he headed into town to the gas station or post office. My son worked with Joe from junior high school until his freshman year in college began, just as Torre Lynn and Zach and Josh Sampson help him now. He learned to drive a tractor and tinker with mechanics and plane lumber along the way, and like most balers, he learned that until he got his knee into the bales, and he grew into the job a little, that it can be a pretty tough way to make a dollar. But he came to love it, as does Joe, not because it made him rich or developed muscle. He loved it because it was honest work, and he accomplished it with good and honest men.

Now, I'm pretty much done with baling hay. I feel no nostalgic pull to stack a wagon anymore, nor a need to fight bumblebees or black snakes in the barn. Riding a wagon slick with chaff is not unlike surfing, as is riding atop a load back to the barn. I remember that we often piled bales so high that we had to dip under the power lines that crossed the road. I know that I've grown too lazy to do what I once did for 75 cents an hour and a slice of pie from Tommy Wilson's wife's kitchen window. It was that delicacy that made a hot day with low pay a little more bearable.

In the meantime, Joe and his crew will continue to bale hay, and they'll continue to wash the chaff from their scratched arms with a hose after sticking a wagonload in the loft. They'll keep fighting the heat and the bugs and the itch and the thunderstorms and the expected mechanical failures of broken wire and busted bales.

True love often comes to us the hard way.

Walking the extra mile for simple beauty September 24, 2007

Just a few weeks ago I read Ed Breen's "A Country Walk" for the third time in just a matter of months. Breen has spent considerable time looking for the extraordinary among the commonplace along a little stretch of country road in rural Grant County.

"What is remarkable about this journey," Breen writes of his two-mile walk, "is how unremarkable it is. It lives only in its specificity; the places and names and faces along this road. It is merely an asphalt thread; a single strand woven into the web of roads across the ninety-two counties of Indiana."

He might as well have been writing about my own sliver of chipped-and-sealed back road, a stretch of pavement that I walk—often with my wife—in the evenings after a day of papers and grades and lessons and books has weighed upon our shoulders and cluttered our heads with cobwebs.

I have written of my walks here often enough—perhaps too often to suit some—but I keep returning to the subject, just as I do that dusty, weed-lined ribbon of road, because it gives me a peace and quiet that I find in very few places.

Each night, often before we even think of supper on the table or of unfinished chores, we walk a few miles.

We gossip a little, as long-married couples are known to do, talk of our kids and families, of places we'd like to go, of places we've been. More often than not, we just listen to the crunch of the pea gravel under our feet and watch our shadows lengthen as we squint into the sun on the trip out and feel it on our backs as we return home. It is a quiet companionship that gives us both time together and time alone. Until the winter weather drives us inside for a while, we take comfort in the sound of our nearly synchronized footsteps and windblown hair.

Despite the return of the summer's heat last week, our walks along County Road 900 South have lately been in anticipation of autumn. It is a spectacularly simple place, lined with fields of corn and beans that have yet to give up their yields. I'd like to think that I thought of the line, but my poetic mate says she thinks the rattle of the brittle, sandpaper-like leaves of the drying corn sounds as if the plants are clapping in a skinny standing ovation for the bountiful harvest and the coming fall. I think its rustling in the breeze is a sad sound, as if the corn knows its time has come.

To most people, I expect the weedy ditches along our road are itchy and boring places. Itchy, they may be, but in no way are they dull. They teem with life, with an abundance of caterpillars and crickets, walking sticks and spiders, all playing out their lives in desperate, dramatic ways. And growing up and around the remnants of long-neglected fences are sassafras and shagbark hickory, shingle oak and black walnut, ash, hackberry, redbud, and locust trees, each taking a turn at pulling a magician's cloak over their changing colors.

At our leisurely pace, we see the delicate purple blooms of crown vetch, the pinkish flowers of late-blooming Sweet William, full-headed stands of goldenrod, the white daisy-like asters, and the lavender burr haircuts and prickly stems of bull thistle. The honeysuckle is past its prime now, and the leaves of creepers and clovers and wild onions and foxtails grow rustier and more haggard with each passing day, yet they add to the color that lines the roads. We see it because it's not reduced to a blur through a passing car window. It's hard to notice such things at 50 miles an hour.

The Johnson Grass, a pest to local farmers, is (at least in its infancy after several summer haircuts) a pretty weed, and if we look close enough, particularly when we have to step off the shoulder of the road to let two cars pass abreast, we see tiny blooms of yellow primrose and recently sheared Queen Anne's Lace, but we hope we can avoid their neighboring red leaves of poison ivy.

Butterflies flit in and out of our country walk, too. In a single evening, we spotted a pair of monarchs, a few swallowtails, and two or three more varieties that won't sit still long enough for us to register their images in our minds until we can get home to look them up in our field guides. Dragonflies too, built like miniature bombers, dip and dive between the heads of weeds as if avoiding enemy ack-ack. The grasshoppers, more abundant this year, I think, often wait until we are almost on top of them before they leap to play a game of chicken or double-dare with us.

I know I'm being a bit romantic here. It's just a few miles of blacktop, and I often suspend my disbelief while I walk each day. The roadsides are littered with the trash of fast-food restaurants and mini-marts, garbage too easily thrown from car windows. What has blown from the open beds of trucks is there; cigarette butts and smokeless tobacco cans, and the ever-present plastic soda bottles, beer cans, and grocery bags are there, too.

But, in spite of the trash, there's a stand of woodland sunflowers near an old concrete corner post. Their bright yellow flowers—often referred to as Jerusalem artichoke—are flashy and bright. It is said that Lewis and Clark ate their roots on their journey west and that now they are sold in health food stores. We see them as a kind of bright farewell to the long summer.

As we crunch along, we often scare up the occasional mourning dove or skittish killdeer, their unique but startled voices all part of the chorus we hear in the country. But one clear evening last week, we saw a blue heron, its stork-like legs half-submerged in the shallows of a pond we pass on every trip we make down the road. It lifted off the water like a hang-glider from a beach dune, and we stopped long enough to watch it disappear from sight.

Our trips may be uninspired monotony to some who see us each evening from their cars or living room windows, but how remarkable this common place is to us.

Going once, going twice, sold...
November 5, 2007

I went to an auction a few Saturdays ago, something I haven't done in years. I came away with an old wooden box of muddy canning jars, an even older iron coffee grinder, and a 1928 Montezuma High School yearbook, the latter an object of desire that I simply couldn't pass up from the moment my wife and I read of it in the sale bill that ran in our county newspaper. Overall, I was pretty pleased with my morning treasure hunt.

My buddy, Joe, is a regular at these sales, often hauling boxes of bolts, old lawnmower parts, used extension cords, and rusty pipe fittings home. He sometimes smuggles his stash past his wife as if she's a border guard when all she really wants is for him to show some restraint in his accumulation of things that "could come in handy." I've been known to use Joe's fabled workshop as my own personal hardware store, so I encourage him to continue his quest for this and that and the other as much as he pleases. We often speak in hushed tones of his latest acquisition or miraculous find lest Linda overhears us discussing a Briggs and Stratton carburetor or copper tubing cutter or some practically new drill bits.

Auctions are true studies in human psychology. Certainly, they can be displays of our weakness to buy things that we don't actually need or can't possibly use. After all, it is a mighty hard thing to turn down an entire cardboard box of chipped glassware, greasy hand tools, or mismatched placemats when it can all be had for a dollar.

But auctions can also give us the triumphant feel of curbing a desire to recklessly spend too. "No, that's too rich for my blood," I told myself more than once as I stopped bidding on an ancient Remington Sure Shot box or pickle crock or picture frame, none of which I had in mind to buy before I stumbled across them as they forlornly sat on or under tables of sawhorses and plywood.

I came to one sure conclusion after going to that sale; we truly don't get to take much with us when we go. We spend our time accumulating years of possessions, only a little of which our children will want or need when we are gone. But sooner or later, at least some of what we had will end up being sold at the barking of an auctioneer's call or simply will be thrown away.

As much as I enjoyed picking through that odd assortment of caned chairs, antiquated television tubes, door knobs, and garden tools, I felt a little sadness knowing that someone once owned and used those things, that their old photographs and letters and dishes were sold for the highest bid. It was as if their memories and anniversaries and birthdays were thrown into those boxes too.

But melancholy can only last so long where bargain hunting is concerned, and my wife was on the trail.

She immediately spied several pieces of Corningware she needed, particularly since she had recently broken a dish when it slipped through her soapy fingers. Her mother and our daughter profited from her largesse, as well.

There were sales at both ends of the building on that gray day, and everything from a car to clothes to can openers went on the block. I wandered the aisles between the sale tables like a kid in a candy store, and in fact saw a number of things that took me back quite a few years. Nothing did that more than a box of Noma Bubble Lights, the elongated Christmas tree lights that seemed to boil after the bulbs sufficiently warmed. We had a set of those lights on our tree when I was a boy, and seeing their bright oranges and reds and greens, and smelling the scent of a freshly cut evergreen tree, were among my favorite things about Christmas. Had the lights been in better shape, I undoubtedly would have bought them.

I found a stack of old records there too. They were ancient LPs and the pile held the faces of Bing Crosby, the Ray Conniff Singers, and Tom Jones, all frozen in time in their over-sprayed hair, incongruous plaids, and hideous shoes. My wife had seen the stack on her trip past the tables as well, and when we met as the bidding wars started, we almost mentioned at the same time that we should buy the Tom Jones album as sort of a joke for our son, Evan, who had inexplicably taken a liking to the Welsh singer after being forced to listen to my oldies radio station on the way to school in his predriver's license days.

But soon we were engrossed in the buying and selling, the auctioneer, Doug Brown, loquaciously moving through tables filled with lamps and Tupperware, punch bowls and knickknacks with an admirable enthusiasm. I soon learned that to scratch my nose, run my hand through my hair, or to even move too quickly meant the potential purchase of a rug or teapot or vacuum cleaner. I talk for a living, but I'm a mere piker by comparison to Doug.

As the morning waned, so too did our enthusiasm. We had groceries to buy and leaves to rake and a walk to take, so we paid our tab and headed for the door. But before we left, my brother-in-law, Gene Baxter, who's familiar with the scent of a good buy himself, walked up to me and handed me that stack of old records, Tom Jones' toothy smile greeting me from the top of the pile.

"I saw these and thought you might want them for Evan," he said with a grin.

Winter has passed, but at a price
March 23, 2008

Despite the windy and wooly winter we've just had, the brown leaves of a scarlet pin oak I planted in my front yard years ago stubbornly hang in defiance of a spring that is now on our doorstep. They'll not drop for a while yet. Only when the breezes turn from the south, and we can be outside in shirt sleeves again for good, will the tiny hands of the oak's new leaves nudge their crunchy neighbors off of the available limb space.

That time is rapidly coming; the weatherman, not always the most accurate harbinger of what's happening outside our doors, has suggested that a few warmer days are on their way to us again this week, and like last, just a handful of hours of sun has been enough to push the crocuses up through the soil and the maple trees to sprout round, red buds.

Spring may have sprung last week as far as the calendar is concerned, but we all know that winter can still rear its ugly head and take one last bite or two out of us before it's done. As I write this, it is a gray and drizzly day, the lingering flipside of the green grass and blue sky times that we know are coming. Despite its vindictiveness, I have seen true signs that the winter has now passed and is being swept away like the gravel we'll push-broom out of our garage doors in spring cleaning.

It seems to me as though the winter creeps up on us, gradually. I rake leaves for weeks in the fall, hauling them a tarp at a time to dump over our back hillsides. It takes weeks to clean my gutters and replant mums and to put away all of our flower pots and wind chimes and back deck furniture, and I gradually dig long johns and heavy coats and gloves out of my closet on a need-to-use basis.

But spring just happens. One minute, I am hunkered down into my coat as I walk between car and store, and the next I hear the familiar ping of baseballs being tagged in after-school practices and realize that long-sleeved shirts are a thing of the past. I have already had my left arm haughtily hanging out of my truck window as I've headed home from work. In a few days, I'll be reading box scores on the sports page.

Just today, I noticed that my yard is greening, and doing so in the cool days before a much-maligned forecast of two or three inches of warm spring rain proves true to green it still further. Already, my magnolia tree is thick with a shaggy coat of fuzzy, gray pods that soon will give way to white blooms, then to lime-green leaves. Everywhere, water swirls in brown, muddy ditches, and ponds are full to their brims, while scruffy itinerant packs of starlings are congregating in annoying cackling clans about our yard to talk it all over.

A few days ago, my wife told me she could hear just a solitary peeper frog in the wetlands below our house. He was singing in a party of one, letting his friends, who were apparently still packed and snoozing in the thawing mud, know that they were late in springing their clocks ahead. Yesterday, she heard a choral festival of them; it hadn't taken them long to hop to the bar and join in.

It is interesting to note that what brought all of this to me was not what I saw out of my windows, but what I saw in our hallway. Near our family room, my wife keeps a baker's rack on which she sets a menagerie of decorations according to the season at hand. On it now, awaiting cardboard box hibernation, is a collection of snowmen, some stuffed, some felt, others ceramic. She has picked them up over the years on sale tables and for birthdays, and she puts them out just after she has stowed her fall line of pumpkins and leaves and Indian corn.

The always-smiling little guys sit there all winter, wrapped in scarves and coats, and most have snow boots on their toeless feet and winking eyes of make-believe coal. They, and a nearly three foot tall cousin who lives near the doorway of our living room, will soon be stashed away, their warm-weather absence yet another suggestion of the times.

In 1938, Wayne Barlow, a composer who had joined the faculty of the Eastman School of Music a year before, wrote "A Winter's Passed." Sub-titled "Rhapsody for Oboe and Strings," it is a short, sad, contemplative piece that was based on two Appalachian folk songs: "A Poor Wayfaring Stranger,"and "Black is the Color of My True Loves Hair." On the occasional dark winter evening, I have sat at my desk and read or marked papers in the light of a single lamp, listening to Barlow's melodies. In those times, I have thought that it would take forever for the winter and the cold breeze it stirs up across the stubbled fields by our house to pass. How often I hoped the season would take my space heater and snow shovel and my cracked, chaffed knuckles with it and be gone. Now, it has.

The oak tree that I mentioned earlier was just a twig, a less-than-pencil-thin reed, when my daughter brought it home from school 17 years ago. She was nine and in third grade, and like her classmates, she was given a tree of choice to plant for Arbor Day. In my mind's eye I can still see her as I shoveled a scoop of dirt from the ground. She stood beside me, a watering can in her hands, her feet pinched together at the toes and her hair blowing in the breeze. I remember telling her that oaks grew slowly, so it would be a long time before her tree got very tall. Now, it stands at least twenty-five feet, perfectly broad at its base.

That memory reminds me that a winter's passing brings another, and another, and another and that their going is not always a good thing.

'Where is human nature so weak as in a bookstore?' April 7, 2008

I have a long list of favorite places to be, and ranked just below being at home on a Saturday morning—where I can wear an old t-shirt and blue jeans and not shave until Sunday—is the dollar aisle of an Indianapolis discount bookstore that I visit as often as I can.

A trip there is like a hunt for buried treasure; I never know what I'm going to find hidden in the sands of its crammed shelves. Already bulging with overstock from retail stores, there's always a steady flow of customers through its doors who lug in box after box of old books that they want off of their coffee tables and nightstands and living room bookcases. Its smell of aging paper and ink is as enticing to me as a bakery's open door, and there's always a slight edge to the customers there as they feverishly snatch up that perfect title before a competing bibliophile spies it.

About a week ago I had an hour to kill there, and sure enough, I hit pay dirt. For a buck I found "For the Love of Books," a neat little tome about one of my favorite topics: reading. More specifically, the author is a Boston trial lawyer named Ronald Shwartz—a one-time English major who luckily went on a guilt trip for taking up the study of law after dropping literature mid-way through college. He asked 115 writers to come up with a series of essays in which they discussed the books that in one way or another had changed their lives or influenced their careers.

Shwartz's book isn't new; it was published nearly ten years ago. But it still reads fresh and relevant to me; his introduction alone was more than worth the price I paid. He writes: "Bookstores were, of course, my weakness...I was soothed by the symmetry of aisles and sections; mesmerized by the vast compression of facts, ideas, lives, epochs, travels, and regions of the heart. Books of imperishable charm or painful insights, endless realignments of twenty-six letters—all contained in one impossibly small and dense place, a paradoxical mix of tranquility and sheer explosive potential—as if a bookstore or library can be said to breach some law of physics or create a new one all its own, like a nuclear bomb with good intentions."

He's right, of course. Put me in virtually any other kind of store or shop and I'm keenly frugal, a tough sell, the kind of customer who's not below doing at least a little wheeling and dealing. I take convincing; I'll figure prices by the ounce, pound, or ton, and I'm more than happy when I can save a few dollars by bringing my own truck and weak back and stout son for homegrown delivery service.

But put me in a bookstore and I turn to jelly; it's Christmas and my birthday and "Bombshell Bargain Days" all rolled into one. I have about as much common sense as a man who shops for cars based on the attractiveness of hub caps. The writer/preacher Henry Ward Beecher surely had people like me in mind when he said, "Where is human nature so weak as in a bookstore?"

Books are my addiction. Two stacks of them in my office have now reached between four and five feet high, as tall as the over-filled bookcase they stand before. By the way, I call those columns my "Yet-to-be-read" piles, and as soon as I get done with the book I'm currently reading—a great account by Pulitzer Prize winner Rick Atkinson on the invasion of Sicily and Italy in 1943—I plan to take on the book at the pinnacle of the front pile, Michael Beschloss's "Presidential Courage." Books by David Halberstam and Ken Follett, Frank DeFord and Garrison Keillor, Norman Maclean and Bill Bryson are in the Green Room just below, waiting to go on.

The problem is, I add to those stacks faster than I pull from them. I'm a little concerned that I could end up like 87-year-old Anthony Cima. Shwartz recounted the story of the San Diego retiree who was in his 12-square-foot hotel apartment when an earthquake hit the city. He was buried under the nearly 9,900 hardcover books he had accumulated. The local newspaper's headline about the incident read, "Man Almost Killed by Love of Books."

Actually, the moral of this tale isn't that I need to get rid of books at all; I think I do that often enough. I loan a lot of them to friends and relatives and students, then forget who has them. I also donate a few to the library, even sell some in our annual garage sale. But keeping Cima and those twin towers in my office, as well as the bookcases in our family and living rooms, in mind, it's my hope that the New Madrid fault does no shifting prior to my next attempt to thin the stock a little.

There are some books that are such old friends that I know I will never give them up. Shwartz got me to thinking about my own favorites, the ones that have made a difference in my life, the ones I have returned to like old buddies year after year for advice and adventure and solace. In other words, could I answer the question that Shwartz asked writers such as Dave Barry and Joyce Carol Oates and Ethan Canin?

Hoosier Kurt Vonnegut, who took part in Shwartz's project, wrote to tell him, "Anyone asking a writer a question like yours should own a thumbscrew and a rack." By the way, Vonnegut listed, among others,

Edgar Lee Masters' "Spoon River Anthology," Mark Twain's "Life on the Mississippi," and interestingly, despite his well-known atheism, The Book of Genesis.

For me, well, I hate to make commitments on things like favorite book lists, but mine would be remarkably similar to Vonnegut's, that is if you throw Robert Louis Stevenson's "Kidnapped" and "Treasure Island" into the mix, maybe a little Robert Frost and David McCullough and...

I had to be in Indianapolis again this past weekend, and since it was only 71 blocks away from my original destination—practically next door—I managed to spend a few minutes (actually, it was two hours) meandering through that bookstore like a lazy stream.

I only bought five books. After all, I have the perfect spot for another stack on the other side of my desk. I just hope we don't have any earthquakes.

CHAPTER THREE

THINGS

'Next to a wife whom I idolize, give me a cat' July 25, 2005

"In ancient times, cats were worshipped as gods; they have never forgotten this."
Anonymous

American writer and humorist Mark Twain had a fondness for cigars, big houses, and cats. In photo after photo, we can still see him clinching the first in his jaws, sitting amidst the luxury of the second, and holding the third in his lap.

Several years ago, my family took a summer vacation to New York. We eventually found ourselves in Elmira, where Twain spent much of his time writing in a tiny octagonal cabin his wife had built for him near the rolling hills of his sister-in-law's home, Quarry Farm. In an archive at the small college in town, I saw old snapshots of Twain holding his cats, or sitting in his porch rocker with them, or stroking them as they crawled across his legs or found some comfortable niche on his writing table.

Twain once said, "I simply can't resist a cat, especially a purring one. They are the cleanest, cunningest, and most intelligent things I know, outside of the girl you love, of course."

Geoffrey Ward, Ken Burns, and Dayton Duncan wrote a wonderful illustrated biography about Twain, and through it I discovered that Twain inherited his fondness for cats from his mother, and from his childhood loved having them around him. "Next to a wife whom I idolize," Twain once wrote in a letter, "give me a cat—an old cat, with kittens."

Twain loved to name his cats, something that my family always seems to find a challenge in doing. Among those he bestowed were Lazy, Sour Mash, Buffalo Bill, and a black mother cat he called Satan, and its kitten, Sin.

In the summer of 1906, Twain actually rented three kittens from a farmer's wife near Dublin, New Hampshire, to keep him company as he wrote, and he promised that he'd return the cats to their owner before he left for New York. He named a gray one, Ashes, but called both of the black kittens Sackcloth since, "when you call one, the other is likely to answer, because they cannot tell each other apart."

In later years, when Twain moved to Connecticut, he found it amusing that one of his kittens "likes to be crammed into a corner pocket of the billiard table—which he fits snugly as a finger in a glove, and then he watches the game by the hour and spoils many a shot by putting out his paw and changing the direction of the ball." It was in those last bitter years, after his wife and children had died, that Twain seemed to most need the distraction.

I fancy myself to be somewhat of a writer, and like Twain, I, too, am often accompanied by our family cats in the process, whether I ask for the companionship or not. Just this morning, a gray kitten that my son found orphaned at our church with a broken leg and countable ribs, spent a good deal of time snoozing on a pile of papers on my desk while I worked on my computer. Pip—the name lifted from Charles Dickens' tale of the needy boy in "Great Expectations"—will chase anything that is thrown, flies, or crawls by. He's also taken a liking to the late-night reading sessions I have in bed, and he seems to always want to sit above my head on the pillow as if he's reading right along with me; I think he's faking it.

Of our cats, we've had Arthur the longest. Named after the fabled king, this burly and surly loner was ironically a pathetic runt as a kitten and seemed to be doomed to a short and miserable life, but a trip to the vet, and a healthier number of trips to the feeding bowl eventually helped him expand into the Garfieldesque malcontent that he is today. He often likes to sprawl on the rug near my desk as the morning sun peeks through my blinds and moves across the floor, but Arthur will take only so many well-intended scratches before he inflicts a little pain; attention to him has to be his idea.

George—named after the neurotic character on "Seinfeld"—my daughter's cat, was the off-spring of the kind of homeless stray we see so often here in the country. Unlike Constanza, he is thin and long, and he often likes to knock my trash basket over, dig out the paper, then stare at me through the gaps in his wicker wonderland. He is quiet and clean and even on the hottest of days likes the warmth of the air that drifts out of the front of our refrigerator.

Max—named after the mad servant/director in "Sunset Boulevard"—is, to put it kindly, not the sharpest knife in the drawer. He spends most his day prowling the woods behind our place, has a meow that makes raked fingers on a blackboard sound pleasant, and seems to be fascinated with scurrying through open doors. I am certain that if I were to open the door to a blast furnace, Max would run through it without hesitation. It is this cat that brings to mind the truth in Ellen Berkley's words: "As every cat owner knows, no one owns a cat."

Like Twain, my history with cats has been a long one. A few years ago I found an old black-and-white snapshot of me sitting on the concrete step of my grandmother's house in bibbed shorts and white t-shirt; I am 2 or so, have a mop of white-blond hair, and sport a black eye. I am offering the photographer a little two-toned kitten as if I've had enough of him for a while. I don't think there has ever been a time since when I didn't have a cat, or more accurately put, a cat didn't have me.

When I think of great writing, I think of a passage in "Huckleberry Finn" where Huck considers all the reason he has for turning in his escaped slave friend, Jim, the weightiest of which being that he may burn in hell; after all, he had heard a minister say so. In the end, Huck decides he'll have to take his chances with eternal damnation, because he can't betray his friendship.

I don't delude myself into thinking that I can write

anything like those wonderful words by Twain. I have no Tom Sawyers or Pudd'inhead Wilsons in me. But I can let our cats lie on my desktop or snoop among my papers and books, or I can reach down with a spare foot to scratch their stomachs as they purr under my chair.

With Twain, I have that in common.

'Something there is that doesn't love a wall'
August 28, 2005

It may seem odd to many to think it, but the best thing that my Grandma Blanche ever gave me, besides a hug in her warm Dutch lap, wasn't my Davy Crockett coonskin cap. It wasn't my Daisy air rifle either; it was a hammer.

More than anybody in my family, my grandmother understood that I needed a rock hammer, a real one with a heavy square head and a tapered tine that could be used for digging and splitting soft stone. I wanted to be a geologist then, and not long before she died at only 60, she wandered through a secondhand shop where she found my hammer tossed into a jumbled box of assorted old tools. It couldn't have cost her more than a dollar to two for the whole mess of screwdrivers, thingamajigs, and rusty wrenches, but I wouldn't sell that hammer today for any amount.

I'm not sure I've ever known when and how and why my interest in rocks began. As early as the fifth grade, I bought two Golden Nature Guides, one for rocks and minerals, and the other for fossils. I must have thumbed through those books a thousand times, and I remember that I used to keep them tucked away in a green Army knapsack that I found while snooping in my grandpa's garage. The books were nestled among paper bags, already-read newspapers, a pair of scratched safety glasses, and two skinny aluminum-tubed paintbrushes, all essentials to the young geologist who just might stumble across some important discovery in his own back yard.

That fascination for stone is with me still. Among the treasures I keep stored on my desk and along the sill of the big window that looks out of my house toward the front yard is a mixed and matched collection of conglomerates, crinoids, quartzes, and arrowheads, all picked up as I've walked through plowed fields, dry creek beds, abandoned quarries, and weedy road cuts. My mom once told me that all I needed to be content was a pile of pea gravel and a sack lunch; my wife still finds Indian beads and bits of stone among the lint and spare change in my blue jeans pockets on wash day.

Years ago, at about the time that my daughter was about to make her first appearance in the family, we moved to this corner of Parke County. One of the things I had always dreamed of having near a home of mine was a rock wall, so, just a summer or two later, I borrowed my dad's dump truck, and the two of us drove to a place where stone was sold by the ton, but was loaded by hand. I bought five tons of heavy green-brown creek rock and drove home tired but certain that my wall would become a quick reality.

More than 20 years later, that rock still borders our front porch and sits around flower beds just north of our red barn and south of our garage. There, it houses geraniums and irises, garter snakes and crickets. It took me much of a summer at that, to split the stone and fit it together like ragged jigsaw puzzles. I splintered wheelbarrow after wheelbarrow and stacked the stuff, all in wonder that such a big pile of rock could cover such a little space. And, I swore that as much as I loved rocks, it would be my first and last experiment in stacking it into walls.

Robert Frost once wrote, "Something there is that doesn't love a wall." He believed that they are most often things that isolate us and that nature conspires to break them down by swelling the ground under them in wintertime or toppling them a stone at a time. I wouldn't argue. Each spring, like the two aging neighbors in Frost's "Mending Wall," I rebuild parts of my stone walls, seeing that in some places the winter's rain and ice have washed away the soil behind them or split the rocks through freezing and thawing in ways that my hammer can't.

My kids inherited my passion, at least as long as they've collected rocks and fossils for their 4-H projects. Many of our summers have been working vacations of sorts as we've driven across the state in search of trilobites along highways and for corals in gravel pits. We've found ourselves in exotic-sounding places like English and Sulphur, just stops in the road really. We've waded through the cool shallowness of a creek in Switzerland County, and we've walked in the trickling branch of my father-in-law's farm, all in the hope of finding something special.

Last summer, we built onto our home. On the back of the new addition, a friend who has talent for such things choreographed our labor into a deck that juts into my back yard. When we were finished with the work—made even more difficult by tree roots, hard yellow clay, oppressive humidity, and raiding parties of blood-thirsty mosquitoes that used us as their own personal pincushions—he suggested that we tack lattice under the deck to give it a more finished look. I had another idea.

It had taken me two decades to forget how hard it can be to move stone, to split it and shape it and stack it. I borrowed my friend's wide-bed Chevy truck, found a bargain price on Mansfield sandstone, bought nearly three tons of the stuff, took my son along to help in its loading, and delivered it in a heap in our driveway.

As beautiful as it is with its browns and pinks and grays, the stone extracted a price from me through more than my checkbook. My back ached, the sweat poured out of me in rivers under a sweltering sun, and one knuckle took a bloody beating when a chisel slipped from my fingers. But the rock sits beneath my deck now, fitted into odd-shaped slots and holes, patiently waiting for the wood above it to rot and fall away, and for the man who put it there to be no more than a memory.

In my living room, I keep a battered oak toolbox. Like my hammer, it was secondhand; long ago my dad brought it home for me to keep my growing collection of fossils and rocks in. It isn't often now, but I occasionally snap open its creaky hinges, and paw through the delicate fossil ferns, the chunks of limestone encrusted with ancient snails and clams, the pink granites, the dark gray shales. I have forgotten the names of most of my collection; after all, it's been a lot of years since I read those little books of mine.

But among the tools that I've accumulated over the years, some through inheritance, others through necessity, is that old rock hammer of mine. I think it has some use left in it yet.

Christmas tree hunt wasn't always a holiday
December 19, 2005

When my kids were younger, my wife and I always made sure that we made the time on a weekend in early December to take them to a Christmas tree farm nearby so we could choose a nice tree together. We didn't always find it, but we had fun trying.

One of the things I loved about that day, besides the fact that we were together and that it was occasionally snowing, was that we would often stand around a fire at the farm and eat a toasted marshmallow or two before we took our tree home to decorate. I'm not going to try to come off here like those days were reminiscent of an episode of "Leave It to Beaver," and I was an amiable Ward Cleaver. As a matter of fact, our adventures often came off a little more like a scene from "Christmas Vacation," with me being the bumbling Clark Griswold.

On that special day, we'd all shove ourselves into my pickup truck, drive the four cramped miles to the farm in our boots and scarves and bulky jackets, walk the trail back to the trees, and begin a search that often rivaled the treasure-hunting nuttiness Ethel Merman and Phil Silvers endured in "It's a Mad, Mad, Mad, Mad World." We wandered the neat grids of trees as a quartet, in pairs, and as loners, calling out to each other when we found that perfect Scotch pine or Douglas fir.

We'd often be there for a couple of hours, tempers sometimes running a little short, and we'd all end up a bit tired and cold and wet, especially when the tree we chose was as far away from the sales shed as was geographically possible.

One year we quickly found what we all considered to be the perfect tree. After dropping myself down into the slush, inspecting the tree from top to bottom and employing the bow-shaped pruning saw, we dragged the tree back to the shed, where they shook the dead needles out of it and prepared to wrap it in a cloak of red plastic netting.

But when they shook our tree, it disintegrated; what appeared to me to be a large secondary trunk was, in fact, a second scrawny tree. What we had left after the quake was a Charlie Brownesque twig that had the employees and a few cocky tree shoppers snickering. I felt like a blockhead. By the way, I remember that the good folks at Fortenberrys' tree farm gave us another shot at finding our tree; we did so, despite real fear that we were all suffering from hypothermia. I don't think it's a coincidence that my wife collects Peanuts tree decorations.

Christmas trees in our house must be relatively short. The man who built our modest place was very nice, but was by no means tall, so our ceilings reflected his vertically challenged design; no vaulted, sky-lit domes in our place. But we made a commitment to real trees after a few years trying an artificial one, and we did so knowing live trees were more inconvenient, that they drop needles and need water and make a mess both coming in and going out. My wife and I grew up with real trees, and that's what we want; it's a tradition.

When we get our tree home, I dutifully cut an inch or two off its base so it will take a deep drink for itself, plant it in our tree stand, and walk it through the front door into our living room. When my daughter was very little, we found every decoration and bulb within her sticky little fingers' reach on the floor one day where she'd played with them all. It wasn't a big deal, but we soon learned that at least until we broke her of the habit, we'd have to childproof the thing. We still have a few of those decorations, glued and taped together for old times' sake.

One of the most memorable tree episodes came about 10 years ago. I had performed my usual crummy job in the tree selection department, and we were enduring the consequences of trying to keep a lopsided tree upright. After shop-vacuuming water off of our carpet a time or two, I thought I had the thing anchored down pretty well, but Murphy must have thought otherwise.

On a cold, dark morning in which we were all heading out the door for a bus trip to Chicago, the tree came crashing down. My kids still rib me a bit about this, because I didn't exactly pause for a few moments and consider what Ward might have done. Instead, I grabbed the tree—lights, decorations, stand and all—and chucked it out onto our front porch like a sack of feed. No, we didn't open presents in parkas; I eventually hacked, chopped, and trimmed the thing into some semblance of verticality, but I will tell you that when it came time to dispose of that particular tree, I did so with impunity.

Last year, my daughter's cats—yes, including the one who required the now-infamous swamp rescue—knocked our tree over a half a dozen times. Needless to say, Martha Stewart would have been appalled at what was left of it by Christmas Day.

As my kids have grown up, we've lost that special day we used to go cut our Christmas tree. We still have a real tree, but after a few transitional years when we went to a lot in town and chose a nice tree together, I now usually pick one up myself since everyone else is so busy. I have to admit, I'm pretty good at eyeballing the lumber now.

We own a few acres of woods, and someday I'd like to plant a nice-sized patch of it in Christmas trees, not to sell to other folks, but just so we can watch them grow, and maybe have a few for our grandkids to cut and decorate in early December. I can't think of a more peaceful place than a grove of evergreen trees. It seems that when the snow falls on them the noises of the world just fade away.

Finding and cutting our Christmas tree hasn't always rivaled a Currier and Ives print on a greeting card commercial. I haven't spotted any Clydesdales, and no one in our home can stand eggnog. But my wife does a nice job of decorating our place, and when I turn on the few strings of lights I hang from the eaves (no, I don't use the staple gun), and we burn a little split sycamore wood in our old farmhouse fire place, we feel pretty warm and content and fortunate every Christmas.

I like our trees, too, even the crooked ones.

A ride back in time with an old blue pickup
January 9, 2006

The old blue pickup truck came toward me as I stood alongside the road at my mailbox in the rain of a drizzling Indiana winter day last week. I didn't notice the driver much, but as the creaking relic cruised by, the breeze of its passing pulled recollections from me of another time.

Like the ice that lingers in the warmer spring air under the stone outcroppings of the rocky hillsides near a creek north of my home each year, I have special places reserved in my memories for things like that truck, and for people like my grandfather, who owned one just like it many years ago.

Most grandfathers are special; mine must have read the job description. There was no truer timepiece than his old truck's tailgate chains clanking to the beat of a rutted driveway as he rattled his way up the hill next to our house on the way to his. He worked the "hoot owl" in those days, and I admired him for his labor, his honesty, and for his love of things outdoors.

In the spring of 1970, just a year or so after he retired, my grandmother died, and heartbroken Grandpa Roy decided that I would be his new traveling companion on his annual pilgrimage south to the mountains of Tennessee and Virginia. I was skinny and 13, and those were the times with him that I treasure most to this day.

My grandfather's truck was "new" to me then, quite modern when compared to the '53 short bed that my dad drove off to construction sites each day. Always careful to have the wheel bearings packed, the wooden bed black with creosote, and the oil changed, my grandfather proudly stood alongside that truck for photos with grandkids, coon dogs, and strings of fresh bluegill.

Particulars of our trips are as misty to me now as the heavy air that hung over the Smokies, but I remember that year after year he improved the truck's creature comforts for our adventures.

For our first trip, we simply "roughed it" by sleeping on musty foam pads rolled out in the bed, a few sheets of corrugated roofing over our heads. By the second year, my grandfather had built a camper shell of his own, and installed a pair of fenderside bunks that made things easier on us. He eventually bought a manufactured camper—still pretty crude by today's standards—but we had a stove, an "icebox," and a door that locked.

The latter became pretty important to me because "Pa" wasn't particular about where he stayed for the night. More than once I thought the coal trucks that owned the little Kentucky highways we traveled would blow us off the roadside as we snored away the night at some rest area or on a wide shoulder. After a day of driving—"exploring," he called it—I'm not sure anything could have kept us awake for long anyway.

We visited distant relatives in Virginia every year, but that wasn't the sole purpose of our trips. My grandfather pumped the clutch and ground the gears and tested all six cylinders of that truck every foot of the way to show me clear mountain streams, to teach me how other people lived, to watch me look for my own breath in the deep hollows of cool rock rarely touched by the sunlight of hot July days.

We came to understand one another in that old truck. I can still see him, his right hand in a firm grip on the silver steering wheel worn black in places by use, humming his favorite old hymns, thinking out loud. He'd often slow the truck to a crawl, the tires scratching in the gravel along the roadside, and with his left hand he'd point out some spot in the distance of a valley below, a hillside plot of tobacco, a mossy ledge of rock, an old iron bridge.

In those moments he'd often mention my grandmother, how she loved those spots, how she used to sit in one particular stream just south of Gate City, Virginia, her pink feet swishing through the cold water as she listened to it gurgle as it fell from stone. I remember one time, that as we stood and looked out across those green hills, my grandfather, his chin in his hand and his elbow on his knee, mentioned in passing that he knew he wouldn't make many more trips, that we all had to grow and go our own ways.

As much as I've tried, I can't quite remember what happened to the truck after Pa died in 1979. It didn't seem so important at the time that it was only used to move the occasional pile of dirt or worn-out freezer. For the most part, it sat in his unused garage and was eventually sold. Now it seems odd that the truck, like his Bible and tools and fishing rods, could have ever been used by anyone else.

That truck couldn't replace the man who taught me how to use an axe or plant a row of corn or to sit in the patient silence of a strip mine pond, but I don't think it was by coincidence that I bought my first truck just a few years after he was gone: a blue, six-cylinder Chevy.

I'm sure a stubborn old fly fisherman I once knew would have approved.

There's a price to pay for progress
January 30, 2006

Just up the road from our place, there used to be an old green clap-board house that had a wrap-around porch heavy with bric-a-brac; it was long on character. The house stood empty for years, and I often wondered as I drove by how much longer it could last, sitting there day in and day out forlorn and lonely and neglected.

I got my answer one day last week; the house that was there in the morning as I made my way to work was gone by late afternoon when I drove home, a bulldozed pile of smoldering kindling and well-chewed earth sitting in its place.

Less than a mile on up the pavement a barn used to stand years ago, a huge, gray poplar masterpiece that didn't appear to be leaning or leaking to me. What was left of it after a few days of demolition was either sold or burned.

I can't tell you that I know that the house could have been saved or whether the barn was in worse shape than could have been seen from a passing car, and I'm not passing judgment on their owners, either. After I did a story about a neighbor who was working to save his old barn from the elements, a farmer friend of mine told me that he wanted to save one of his antique barns, but simply couldn't afford to sink tens of thousands of dollars into a structure that could be replaced by a metal building for much less. It didn't make him happy to see the barn go, but it was a matter of keeping his head above rising financial waters.

There's little doubt that the house I now live in will someday face the same fate. The man who built it was a proud, do-it-yourself kind of guy who used a good bit of second-hand, rough-hewn farmhouse lumber to build the place as sturdily as he could. I have often wondered how and why he engineered some of the things in the house the way he did, but someday, I am certain, another owner will wonder the same thing of me.

I have worked hard to repair and replace and improve on what he did, but the integrity of my house was first given to it by him, not me, and most of its distinguishing marks are his off-spring as well. My wife and I may live in the house longer, but it was put here through his spirit and vision.

The permanence of things is measured by the people who outlive them, and I will not outlive my house. The old lady who used to live down the road might have had that same thought of her house before she passed on, and I can't imagine that she dreamed of the day that it would be pushed into a pile of rubble.

I believe we have a difficult time comprehending real things, of places and spaces made with the hands of a higher being instead of union labor or willing weekend warriors. We have become obsessed in this country with putting up new things, tearing down the old, and like beliefs and virtues, houses and barns are lost as we replace them with what we see as new and improved.

Just how many acres of farmland are we going to give up to build more convenient drug stores, pizza places, and gas stations?

Among Thomas Jefferson's interests and hobbies were "putting up and tearing down," his passions for architecture. I've been twice to his home in the hills of Virginia, and I believe that much more of the man is in that house than in the grave that lies two stone throws away under a marker he designed himself. The beauty of that house in the Blue Ridge makes me feel all the more for the craftsmen and the calluses spent in building that clapboard house and cavernous barn along a country road in Indiana.

The native, rough timber that serves as the skeleton of my house, its tiger oak fireplace, and the ancient pie cupboard that sits with me near my desk, came from other houses to live with me in mine. Those and the scraps of my life, the books and pictures, the rocking chair and cedar chest, have places in our hearts. Some of them will eventually go to spend time with one or the other of my children.

My wife and I are guilty as charged; we too wish we could build a new house someday in the woods near the venerable farmhouse her parents own, but I hope that I will not have to face the look of this house as it stares at the bulldozer or wrecking ball.

As I drove home past the splintered house and the ghost of the barn a couple of days ago, a trio of Canadian geese, their gray-flecked bellies and nose-coned beaks plain to see, passed overhead in the air of an unusually warm January day, gliding without concern over the power lines and pine trees below. They had undoubtedly spent a while on the pond just down the hillside from our house and were taking off to see a little of the world.

I hope that's something that will never change.

The most revolutionary three minutes on TV April 3, 2006

As much as I don't like to admit it, I'd say I've watched my fair share of television over the years. My parents never used it as a babysitter, and I can remember seeing my mom whisking through our living room dozens of times, slapping off the set with a quick left jab and telling me, "It's too nice of a day to be sitting on the couch watching that thing. Get outside and find something else to do."

I'm sure that Mom never heard architect Frank Lloyd Wright call television "chewing gum for the eyes," but I think she'd have agreed with the sentiment.

I did, however, manage some quality TV time on our scratchy gray couch, and I can still see the late night flickers of our old Philco, a Jethro Bodine-sized bowl of cereal in my hands, while I watched "Gunsmoke," "The Twilight Zone," "The Wonderful World of Disney," or "The Andy Griffith Show."

It may sound odd, but I believe that the most daring three minutes ever aired on national television may have come on January 14, 1963. In its third year and in its 77th episode, "The Andy Griffith Show" managed to do something that today no television executive in the country apparently wants to try with a national audience that seems to be more and more addicted to noise and violence and crude humor.

In that innovative scene, the centerpiece of an episode called "Man in a Hurry," Sheriff Andy Taylor, loyal friend, Deputy Barney Fife, and Raleigh businessman Malcolm Tucker sing a few comforting lines from "The Church in the Wildwood." They didn't change a word, didn't pick up the beat, didn't use the moment to preach or pontificate. Nobody flashed any skin; there was no profanity, no cutting edge sarcasm. Just three men on a porch lost in their thoughts humming while one strummed a guitar. I think that despite watching it countless times, my blood pressure still drops a point or two as soon as I hear the tune.

I love "The Andy Griffith Show," grew up with it, and have never outgrown it. Most of its 249 episodes are in black and white, and most of its simplistic but funny plots couldn't have possibly happened. The show was hardly representative of the edginess and anger of the '60s in which it was produced, and the controversies of race and politics and Vietnam didn't seem to be able to cross into Mayberry County, let alone make the 17-mile drive to town from Mt. Pilot.

The show remains on television today, running in endless marathons or coming to us in badly-needed daily doses on a network devoted to nostalgic programming. In the past few years, new DVD sets of the show make it possible to watch anytime we choose. It's still funny, but in many ways, I've found it to be just about the most thought-provoking thing I can watch on the tube these days. I find it that way, not because it forces me to confront the day's headlines or because of its gritty realism. Instead, I use it like an ice pack held against a bruise, like a familiar joke that still makes me grin, like a friend I'm always happy to see.

The world I grew up in was not Mayberry, North Carolina, but it was the early '60s. I did often run down the County Line with my dad to a gas station much like Wally's for an impossibly cold glass bottle of cream soda and to fill up the tank with high test. I did get my hair cut in a place a little like Floyd's, and the little town closest to our house was just about as lazy and friendly as Mayberry was, although I can't say I knew anyone as goofy as Gomer Pyle or who wore the old salt n' pepper quite like Barney, either.

There's more to the show's popularity than aging "Baby Boomers" taking a simple trip down memory lane; one look at a metal Flintstones lunch box or my fourth grade class picture can do that. Respected universities have courses devoted to "The Andy Griffith Show," a myriad of internet sites and chat rooms are available about it, and, according to a monthly on-line newsletter (The Bullet), there are now over 1,700 chapters of The Andy Griffith Re-run Watchers' Club up and running across the country. Trading cards, cook books, and coffee mugs abound as well, but merchandising isn't keeping this show on our televisions every day. It's the show's life lessons.

Richard Kelly, the author of one of the best books on the series, "The Andy Griffith Show" (1982), says, "The series offers a needed parable for our times...the show captures a romantic myth that continues to entice and satisfy our yearning for a simpler world, one filled with love, purpose, respect, laughter, understanding, and a sense of belonging and permanence." Neal Brower, the author of "Mayberry 101," added in 1998, "Imagine a town where one could live peacefully, securely, and happily ... no drugs, no gangs, no violent crimes. If this was a dream back in the '60s, think what a longed-for dream it is in today's world."

Deep down, I think we all yearn to live in a place like Mayberry. We yearn to have a pa like Andy, wish we had friends like Barney or Floyd, wish we could feel as safe and secure as the folks who live in a town where the most serious crime is Emma Watson's chronic jaywalking.

Like any Andy Griffith Show fan, I have a handful of favorite episodes. Who can forget Barney as he zips down Main Street on his motorcycle to set up a "checkpoint chickie," Aunt Bea's toxic pickles, or a "gassed" Otis Campbell riding into town on a cow? It makes me smile to think of the Fun Girls or Winkin', Blinkin', and Nod, Opie's orphaned birds. Can anyone on television today compare to the jug-playing, banjo-picking mountain clan, The Darlings, or to the nutty, rock-throwing malcontent Ernest T. Bass? It's still easy to picture Gomer running down the street yelling, "Citizen's arrest!"

For me, especially when I'm a little blue, I most often return to Andy Taylor's front porch on a warm summer Sunday evening, to a comfortable rocking chair, and to the slightly sad melody of that old hymn.

Many of us hear the call of 'The Blue Whale'
June 5, 2006

My wife and I told my daughter when she was in high school that if she kept her grades up and took care of it, we'd give her our family car when the time was right. When she was a junior, we bestowed upon her our blue 1993 Chevy Lumina, still in pretty good shape despite its mileage. I had always kept it in good repair and its oil changed. It had relatively new tires, a strong battery, and good paint. We told her she'd better take care of it because she'd be buying her next car.

Ellen soon began to call her new wheels "The Blue Whale," and I quit counting the number of trips she made down the road to school for practices and ball games or into town to work at the grocery store. I was always just a little more relaxed when I saw that old blue car pull into our driveway, knowing it had done its job another day. It became a matter of trust.

A high school graduation, an undergraduate diploma, a master's degree, a whole lot of trips into Terre Haute, and nine years later, Ellen finally decided last month to give up the car. It has nearly 180,000 miles on its odometer and needed a few repairs. As our mechanic looked it over not long ago, he asked Ellen, "Now, which sound am I supposed to be listening for?"

My daughter is a kind and unusually loyal soul, and rather than sit the car in the front yard and hang a sign on it asking for the best offer she could get, she wanted to donate it to a local charity. Tears welled in her eyes as I unscrewed its license plate and she handed over the keys. She snapped a photo or two of it and said the car looked lonely by itself in the parking lot. As we drove away I think she understood a little why a captain often chooses to go down with his ship.

We've probably all had a blue whale in our past. My first car was a 1962 Plymouth Valiant that my sister affectionately named "The Bomber." It was a two-tone sedan—I think pitted white and rust brown is two-tone—had only one workable door out of its four, a heater that didn't heat, and a set of red and gray seat covers that looked like plastic shredded wheat.

Even though it was decrepitly ugly, I learned to love that car. Because it had a new set of tires when we sold it, we got $125 for it from a man a county away who wanted "cheap transportation" to work. It had cost only $75 when my dad bought it out of an old lady's barn lot where her cows had spent much of their time butting dents into its fenders. Its other scrapes and bruises had not come from the old gal gingerly driving the thing to church on Sundays, but rather from its frequent trips to the tavern on Friday nights.

I remember that driving the car to school was a

source of embarrassment, especially since a buddy of mine had a brand new candy-apple red Cougar with factory mags, a snazzy vinyl roof, and an eight-track cassette player. I still recall the sting I felt one cool October morning as I inched my way into the school parking lot. A tall blonde girl in bell-bottoms stood on the curb as I crept by, and as she gazed down through my half-raised window glass—it wouldn't go all the way up— she smugly said, "Nice car." I can still see her smirk.

Despite having to get into the back seat and roll over into the front, despite enduring its leaks and hanging head liner and its mouse infestation, I think I learned more from that car than from anything I've ever owned. It was a lesson in humility every time I got behind the wheel. In the winter I was afraid that I would be headed into town at the same time the police were searching for a liquor store robbery suspect, and I would be the guy driving down Third Street wearing a ski mask and gloves...

That first car taught me that working one's way up from the bottom of the ladder isn't always bad. My second car cost me $300, and after it hit 160,000 miles, I sold it and bought a $750 car, then a $1500 truck. I was proud that after my dad's initial investment in that old car, I had been able to take things on for myself, had even learned how to put on a set of brakes and change an alternator.

My first car had a push-button transmission and tail fins. Its hood rattled and threatened to pop open at speeds over 40 miles per hour–which was about as fast as I wanted to drive it anyway. I had to drill holes in its floorboards to let rainwater drain out, got used to scraping the frost off the inside of my windshield, and learned that prayer was answered in those days when drivers had to have their cars pass an annual inspection by a mechanic.

Now, I'm just thankful that Ellen's car lasted as long as it did. I suspect that we'll still see it around town every once in a while, hopefully owned by someone gentle who'll occasionally put a coat of wax on her. For several years after I sold it, I used to see my old Plymouth tooling down Highway 41, each time sagging a little more as its springs atrophied with the passing of time.

Not for a minute do I feel that my daughter or I got a bad deal with our first cars. I think we learned that getting everything we want, when we want it, can be a bad thing. Now, Ellen has "Marge," her new ride, although not brand new. My wife—whose first car was a green and white '57 Ford—and I have forgotten most of the cars we've owned since we were 16.

I don't think any of us will forget "The Blue Whale" though.

Beauty of hollyhocks a testament to persistence June 19, 2006

In the late evening glimmer of a falling June sun, I sat with my thumbs tucked under my chin and watched a hummingbird dash between a feeder under a backyard pine to a stand of deep red hollyhocks that grow on a hillside near our barn.

The birds have always fascinated me, but my life with them came when we first moved to this house. The flowers, however, are a thing from the distant past. I have not outgrown hollyhocks, nor do I wish to.

Earlier this spring I was scrounging through the odds and ends of an unintentional collection on a garage shelf. Nestled among the unmatched gloves, the cans of forgotten paint, and a few old garden tools sat a rusting coffee can, the makeshift home of a sack labeled with my mom's elegant handwriting. "Phyllis' hollyhock seeds," it read.

Smiling, I took the seeds to a then bare spot of soil on the hillside I've gradually carved from our woods, dropped them into the red-brown dirt as if sowing grass, sloshed a half-can of water across the work, and walked away.

Within a few weeks I could see the pale green fans of the tiny plants grabbing the air for sunlight. Phyllis, one of Mom's oldest and dearest friends, has been gone for years now, but part of her is still alive and reaching out of the soil.

The hollyhock has never been a highly respected flower. Its long slender stems came in handy over the years to help hide outhouses and henhouses, junked cars, and trash pits. Hollyhocks were easy to grow, but easier to neglect. Most often, they are biennial; planted one year to flower the next.

Although I neatly trim around my gangs of plants, I have rarely planted or replanted our hollyhocks. Our best stands simply appeared where I had thrown the splotched and bug-eaten carcasses I had cut out of a front yard flowerbed. Their accidental beauty is a testament to the persistence of nature.

From what I've read, hollyhocks (scientific name Athaea rosea) first came to America from China and were once eaten as a pot herb. Its flowers are still used by some as medicines, specifically for chest complaints. Hollyhocks are also used for making dyes, their blooms gathered in July or August and dried in thin layers on trays in the sun.

I suppose that I most remember the pink and crimson blooms growing in Grandma Blanche's flower garden. She always sprinkled hollyhocks among her rhubarb and irises, and often I wandered in bare feet to her back step and caught her leaning amid her flowers pulling weeds and snipping blooms. She wasn't very tall and her head would pop up amidst the hollyhocks, her reddened, chubby face framed in the color of the flowers, not unlike a painting I once saw at T.C. Steele's House of the Singing Winds near Nashville.

Despite the apparent lack of respect, the hollyhock has been cultivated. A good many varieties exist, among them a mixture of white, red, pink, and yellow blooms called Indian Spring. Other variations are called Summer Carnival and Rugosa; I have no idea what our hollyhocks are called.

My wife has spent a life with hollyhocks, too. Her

Grandma Ruth first showed her how to make hollyhock dolls from the flowers when Joanie was a girl still wearing cowboy boots and horn-rimmed glasses and missing a few front teeth. The dolls were intricate sculptures that sat alongside other dolls made of corn tassels and that art was proof that often the most treasured playthings are short-lived but long remembered. My children can claim that in a digital age of special effects and computer animation that they saw their mother sitting at our old oak kitchen table carefully folding and wrapping hollyhock blooms into frail families that lasted just a day or two.

I am confident that someday my wife will get a book about her grandmother and those flowers into print. I am as equally confident that we are headed to a time when the things of the past, whether they be front porch rockers, old-time religion, or playthings made from flowers, will be important to us again. Perhaps as a culture we will someday decide to slow down.

In the heat of southern California, the great architect Frank Lloyd Wright was so impressed with the lowly hollyhock that he built a magnificent house based on the flower's basic structure. Wright believed in the "organic house," that nature's designing power was superior to that of man.

For as much as I would like to say that my yard and garden are my own creations, like Wright, I know better. My best flowers are those accidental hollyhocks, cultivated, not with my hands, but by those of a subtle and awesome power.

When it comes to reading, computers can't beat books
September 18, 2006

I listened to a speaker a few years ago whose topic was the growing role of technology in our lives, and since a good bit of my time is spent finding my way around a computer keyboard, I couldn't disagree with him much. But when he went so far as to tell his audience that someday soon computer screens and e-books would replace real books, and that bookstores were already obsolete, well, those were fighting words.

I don't imagine that I impress many people as a deep thinker, but I am a reader. The heft of a good book in my hands is as satisfying as most things I can wish for. Somehow, I don't think being propped up in bed with a computer screen glowing in my face has quite the same appeal as a good book sitting on my chest or the solid feel of a paperback stuffed in the rear pocket of my jeans.

To wander a bookstore or the library stacks is a joy to me. I know, I could simply look up a book's title at a computer terminal, even reserve copies by Internet, which I do at times. But to while away the minutes, just looking through books, not knowing what I might find, is a diversion almost as pleasant as reading the books I've discovered.

I've loved to read since I was a boy. My mom's bedtime stories, a few inspirational teachers and a decrepit television tuner that only pulled in three fuzzy channels were probably most responsible for it.

As long as I can remember we had books in our house, even at a time when we weren't able to buy much more than groceries. I think my mom was always a little insecure about her lack of a formal education, but she was still one of the best-read people I've ever known, including those on the college campus I roamed for a while. Her education came less from a classroom than from her books and her Bible, and just as Dennis Hanks said of his famous cousin, AbrahamLincoln, she was able to make books "talk to him [her] better than most."

I was also fortunate to find a mate who loves to read; it was surely one of the shared interests that pulled us together, and perhaps has helped keep us together. We didn't exactly read Kafka on our first date—more than likely we took my '71 Duster out for pizza at Pasquale's. I do know that as exasperated as my wife gets with my wanting to build even more bookcases in our house than the ones we already have, and with the stacks of books I leave about my office and on our night table, she has a hard time not piling them up herself. After all, she's a librarian, so I find stashes of her own near our bed or crammed into the remaining spaces of our closet.

Among my fondest memories of grade school were the hand-in-hand walks our class took up the road from Otter Creek Elementary to a branch of the public library. The building was dark and old and musty; its lumpy wooden floors moaned under the weight of its books, and a beat-up screen door did little to keep the dust off the shelves, but wandering that library and having my very own dog-eared library card in my pencil-thin wallet are treasures that I'll not forget.

Historian David McCullough is considerably more eloquent on this subject than I am. Just last week I had my senior students read a speech he gave as he accepted the National Book Award in 1995. He's concerned, as am I, that the Internet, and our growing dependence on computer technology, is changing our very definition of learning.

"The tools for accessing data grow ever more wondrous and ubiquitous and essential if we're to keep in step, we've come to believe," McCullough said. "All hail the Web, the Internet, the Information Highway. We're being sold the idea that information is learning, and we're being sold a bill of goods."

McCullough added, "Information isn't learning. Information isn't wisdom. It isn't common sense. It isn't kindness. Or trustworthiness. Or good judgment. Or imagination. Or a sense of humor. Or courage. It doesn't tell us right from wrong."

In a profession where I spend much of my time begging my students to read, imploring them to just sample the books I keep on the shelves of my classroom, I'm afraid I'm losing the battle. To be sure, some of my students do read, do crave the time they have to enjoy a good book, do allow their imaginations to soar with the words on the pages, but it's precious few, and so many others bring to mind what Mark

Twain, that most adventurous of spirits, once said: "A man who does not read good books has no advantage over the man who can't read them."

On the old classroom bookcase I have, pulled out of the attic of a dilapidated 19th century schoolhouse just before it met the wrecking ball, are Robert Louis Stevenson and Robert Frost, Eudora Welty and Flannery O'Connor, Agatha Christie and Alistair McLean. Some boy or girl's best friends could be on those shelves, if they'd just pick up that one special book.

I consider my books to be friends, and not just in times of doubt or loneliness or crisis, either. They have become a part of my life, living and breathing things, as they sit on my shelves or desktop—my oak roll-top, not the one reserved for my computer—always willing to share with me what they know. I tend to keep the books I like best close by, and like my family and best buddies, they've yet to let me down when I needed a little companionship or advice. They've been with me through sleepless nights, hospital room watchcares, bright days at vacation beaches, stuffed into bags with camping gear, and are often left scattered near my front porch rocker or beneath my family room lamp. Wherever I go, they seem to go, also.

Although I have no idea who said it, I once heard that a good book on your shelf is a friend that turns its back to you but still remains your friend.

It's good that I'm a man with so many friends.

Is it really that nifty to turn 50? September 25, 2006

I turned 50 a few weeks ago. I wasn't humiliated; wasn't upset; I didn't feel like I'd taken a leap toward bulk fiber, soaking my bunions, and wearing my pants under my armpits, either. Because I had promised the same for her, my wife kept my birthday a low-key affair: no black balloons, no childhood photo in the personal ads, no dancing gorilla at my birthday party doing its thing in a G-string (which is exactly what happened when a buddy of mine hit the big 5-0 a few years back).

It's just that I never imagined being 50, and if I'm supposed to feel 50, I don't. I still shoot buckets in the backyard, have all of my teeth, and occasionally listen to other stops on the radio dial besides my usual "oldies" station. I've been known to switch my brand of toothpaste for the heck of it; I am not set in my ways. This dog can learn new tricks.

I know people who have chest freezers as old as I am. The friend I mentioned above has socks that are as old as I am. It's true; I was born during the first Eisenhower administration, I owned a Davy Crockett coonskin cap, and I did think Donovan was pretty cool for a while.

Years ago, and I mean the time when I considered people who were 50 to be fossils, turning the half-century mark really was thought to be getting up there. If you take a quick glance through yearbooks from decades past, some high school seniors looked like they were pushing 50 before they graduated. Of course, that generation also fought World War II and saved democracy...

Just the other day I heard a talking head on the television say that 70 is the new 50, that people just aren't aging like they used to, that older Americans are more active than those who lived a generation or two ago. I have to remind myself of that when I also read medical articles that suggest that mine is the "Twinkie" generation, that obesity is running rampant among us late "Boomers," whose idea of exercise is walking briskly back to the service counter to get our second tray of fries and a refill on our drinks.

I also know that I'll have to go some at 50 to be more active than my grandfather was at 70; he most often whipped the sun out of bed. On too many nights to remember, I used to watch his ancient carbide mining lamp bob its way back into the woods, my grandfather under it with a rifle in his hands to hunt raccoons and shiver himself warm. That light would often not come bobbing back until two in the morning, yet he'd still beat me out of bed come sun-up to work on his roof or pull weeds before the dew was burned off the ground.

I do understand now that there are some distinct advantages to being 50. I just received "valuable" information in the mail from AARP and will be getting free checking at my bank. More young cashiers will call me "Sir," and in just a few more paltry years, I'll be able to cash in on discounted meals, better deals on car tires, perhaps cheaper hotel rates. Of course, all of those discounts will probably be off-set with the bills from my colonoscopies and reading glasses, but at least I'll feel better about it.

I didn't exactly get off unscathed on my birthday. I was at work that day customarily early only to find my classroom decorated with an assortment of the latest in "Ain't it nifty" regalia, complete with black crepe streamers and posters. One of the signs labeled me as "Older than dirt;" another suggested that if I were a car I'd be an antique, and yet another informed me that my motor was still running but my warranty had expired. Rather than be embarrassed, I was kind of thankful; Sue Cleghorn, and her husband, Bob, who were in my room decorating at 11 o'clock the night before made me smile. Besides, they're both older than I am, so I indulged them their insinuations that I too was growing a bit mossy.

A newly-married friend, half my age, told me a few days ago that her mother thought her 50s were more fun than her 40s; her children were raised and she had more time to do some of the things she wanted to do. I hope to agree with her, but one thing I won't do is get myself used to calling 50 "middle aged." As crotchety 79-year-old Norman Thayer Jr. told his wife in "On Golden Pond," after she suggested they were a middle-aged couple: "People don't live to be 150."

But there's no need to conserve my energy yet; I don't get winded playing chess, haven't had an urge to wear black socks with my sandals, haven't been stumped by the word search in Modern Maturity magazine. I don't even like the word "age." Cheese ages; I've simply matured. I heard it said once that reaching my age is when you start seeing how long your car will last instead of seeing how fast it will go. I'm just more experienced now, that's all.

I have a number of friends who are much older than I am, but I don't consider them old at all. They may be pushing 80 or so, but I see Buck and Carolyn, and Ted and Chuck, among others, almost every morning on a treadmill at the Wellness Center working up a sweat. Older friends like Perry Huxford and Morris Garrigus mow their own yards and trim their own trees. My buddy, Murray Melton, may have had heart surgery, but if there's an 80-year-old body with a kid trapped in it, it's his. Those folks lead active lives; the kind I hope to have. They inspire me to keep working, to keep moving, and to keep a sense of humor. The stereotypes of aging that I've mentioned here with tongue in cheek, simply don't apply in their cases.

Like them, I have no intention of letting this little milestone slow me down at all. I'm going to keep taking my vitamins, keep pushing myself away from the table after my first plateful, and I'm going to continue to take those long walks in the evening and do my push-ups too.

As a matter of fact, I'm going to do all of those things tonight...just after my nap.

For all of those "wonderful people out there in the dark" October 23, 2006

A few weeks ago, just for an instant, I flashed back to a day when my mom took me downtown to eat a burger and drink a frosty mug of root beer at a long, dark restaurant that sat inviting and cool on Wabash Avenue. I may not remember the name of the place, but I can recall the heavy lacquer on our booth's benches, the whir of the ancient ceiling fans, and how I shoveled hot, fat French fries into myself until my plate was as clean as the ones that sat in newly-washed stacks under the countertop.

After the feast, we walked to the movies under a wilting sun, not down the street to The Grand, but over to The Indiana, a few blocks away. We watched "The Moon-Spinners" with Hayley Mills; Donald Duck was the opening cartoon act. I can still see Mills' blonde hair blowing in the breeze some 45 years later, can hear the creak of the windmill that was the key to the mystery in the story, and can feel the warm glow of the red lights that lined the theater's walls as the two of us sat there hunkered down in our seats. It may have cost us 50 cents apiece to watch the show.

I loved the movies then, and I love them now, and I imagine that just about everyone reading this can remember a moment like mine when they've experienced the magic of a dark movie theater. In those days, my mom used to take me to the movies as a special treat, perhaps on a day when pants were on sale at Smith's, or maybe when I had to face the dentist, who didn't seem to be as gentle then as they are now.

That love for movies is the reason why I feel so fortunate to teach a film class. I want my kids—both the two we've raised, and those who sit in my classroom every day—to love movies too, not just because films can teach and entertain us, but because, as Turner Classic Movie's host Robert Osborne says, they can inspire us too.

I read an article Osborne wrote for "Guideposts Magazine" this summer. In it he recalled the years he spent growing up in Colfax, Washington, during the '40s and '50s, and how he got his first job working at the Rose Theater there. He said that the theater was "a doorway to another dimension," a description with which many of us can probably identify.

Times have changed since those days for Osborne at The Rose. They've changed for me from the time when I walked, ticket in hand, toward the uniformed usher at The Indiana too. Although there are exceptions, I don't feel movies are as good as they used to be. I often see films that entertain me; I rarely watch newer movies that inspire me.

Osborne's time at The Rose taught him quite a bit about human nature and the power of movies. He wrote, "Throughout my young years in Colfax, the movie house was second only to church as a place to get your bearings—to find the strength to live, no matter what life threw at you, to set your moral compass."

I'm not sure I want my kids to set their moral compasses by what Hollywood is cranking out these days. Don't get me wrong; there are many good films being made now, and new technology has enabled us to see unbelievable special effects, but I always seem to return to classic films when I want to feel better about humanity, and apparently Osborne does, too.

"For me, the movies I introduce each night [on TCM] aren't just wonderful entertainment. They're old friends: friends that did more than just show me, as a young boy in Colfax, what the world was like. They showed me how best to live in it," he wrote.

Osborne went on to list 12 films that inspired him, and among them are a few of my favorites: "Mrs. Miniver," "To Kill a Mockingbird," "It's a Wonderful Life," "Ben Hur," and an inspiring little movie starring Joel McCrea that I saw for the first time just a year ago, "Stars in My Crown." The newest film he mentioned was "Field of Dreams," which would make my list, too.

Osborne also mentioned that as an usher at The Rose, one of his jobs was to clean up when the lights came on, but he said that job was pretty easy because there were no concession stands then. "After all, people didn't come to the movies to eat. Or talk! Television hadn't ruined people's manners in that regard. And, of course, there were no cell phones going off. The theater was almost a sacred place. No one would have thought about profaning it with food and chitchat," he said.

I'd be willing to trade my buttered popcorn right now for mannered, quiet, cell-phoneless audiences at the movies anytime.

When I think of the films that inspire me, I have to admit that they're the ones we watch in class because I want my kids to feel the same way I do when the movies flicker to life on the screen, mostly in black and white. Charlie Chaplin's "Modern Times" encourages me in tough times; Frank Capra's "Mr. Deeds Goes to Town" renews my faith in the integrity of the average Joe; "The African Queen" inspires me to tackle tough jobs; "Lilies of the Field" makes me feel I'm living where I am supposed to be; "The Maltese Falcon" and "The Treasure of the Sierra Madre" show me what greed can do to people.

My list of favorite movies, movies that inspire me, is long, perhaps even longer than Osborne's. From Mr. Chips to Rick Blaine, Rhett Butler to Tom Joad, I know that movies, and their characters, don't have to be loud or violent or sleazy to be good.

I've taken to heart something I heard once, in an old movie that I watched one night in the dark of my early-morning living room. It's called "How Green Was My Valley," and in it, a man named Huw Morgan looks back at his life as a boy in Wales. He says, "There is no fence or hedge around time that is gone. You can go back and have what you like of it, if you can remember."

How could I ever forget a movie like that?

A winter night's trip to 'Treasure Island'
February 19, 2007

It was on one of the coldest nights of the year last week when I decided to grab a book from my hope-to-read-soon pile and headed for the warmth of my bed and my great-grandmother's quilt. I had spent some time outside that evening and had witnessed a dusk as beautiful as a frameless Rockwell Kent landscape, and my frosty breath had seemed to freeze in mid-air like the dust of some distant nebula.

The book I picked up was called "Deep Blue," a collection of stories about shipwrecks and treasure and lonely survivors of catastrophes at sea. It is the kind of book I enjoy most, for I am a man with more imagination than intestinal fortitude, particularly when it comes to being the kind of adventurous soul like those whose stories were told page by page as they took to the sea.

Among the tales of Patrick O'Brian and Farley Mowat and Herman Melville was a lengthy excerpt from Robert Louis Stevenson's "Treasure Island," a book I first read as an illustrated classic in grade school. It is a great, great book, and seeing that it had been years since I opened up the adventure story of young Jim Hawkins, the dying Billy Bones, and the conniving Long John Silver, I decided to warm my feet on flannel sheets while conducting a lamp-lit adventure of treasure maps and cutlasses and courage rather than skip to the selections I had never read. I think before I could even read well, I treasured "Treasure Island." Among the set of white World Book encyclopedias and dusty National Geographics and book-of-the-month selections that my mom faithfully ordered was a very old copy of Stevenson's classic that had been around our house since the beginning of my memory. Although not illustrated by the great N.C. Wyeth, whose work with Stevenson's stories helped make him an artistic success, the old tome was highlighted by a half-dozen color plates depicting the shipwrecked Ben Gunn, the aristocratic Dr. Livesey, and a scared young Jim as he hid in the apple barrel listening to Silver's plans of mutiny.

I have seen some of Wyeth's work with "Treasure Island," and I truly believe that when I read the book, it is his Old Pew I see blindly staggering down the road swinging his stick, his Jim leaving home as his mother pulls her apron to her eyes, and his hoisting of the skull and crossbones from the decks of the Hispaniola. In some ways, "Kidnapped" and "The Black Arrow," both from Stevenson's pen too, are Wyeth's, as well.

The story goes that it was Stevenson's stepson who inspired "Treasure Island." The great Scot, born in 1850, had gained little success as a struggling playwright. He was 30 years old when he found the boy wiling away a cold rainy day with a box of paints and the drawing of an island he had imagined. Stevenson helped his son expand the map, and soon Skeleton Island and Spyglass Hill, and eventually, an entire book, was born.

In one of my favorite scenes from the film "On Golden Pond," the crotchety old Norman Thayer Jr., after learning that a young houseguest has never read "Treasure Island," tells him to go upstairs to tackle the book; Norman wanted a report over the first chapter the next morning. The old professor may have been an incurable curmudgeon, but he believed that every boy—probably every girl too—should read "Treasure Island," an opinion with which I wholeheartedly agree.

Take, for instance, Jim's account as he and his mother escape their inn with Bones' map seconds before the bloodthirsty pirates arrive: "Next moment we were both groping downstairs, leaving the candle by the empty chest; and the next we had opened the door and were in full retreat. We had not started a moment too soon. The fog was rapidly dispersing; already the moon shone quite clear on the high ground on either side...the sound of several footsteps running came already to our ears, and we looked back in their direction, a light tossing to and fro and still rapidly advancing showed that one of the newcomers carried a lantern."

Stevenson's words helped me smell and feel the salt air and cool breezes on my own face, which I'm certain would have been beading sweat.

Before I fell asleep on that star-filled, black-blue night, my head filled with beach sand and muskets and treasure chests, I remembered something that Walt Disney, who had a pretty good imagination himself, once wrote. He said, "There is more treasure in books than in all the pirates' loot on "Treasure Island" and at the bottom of the Spanish Main, and best of all, you can enjoy their riches every day of your life."

How right he was.

The summer of love: A man and his mower
April 9, 2007

As uneasy as it makes me feel, I have to admit that I've just recently begun to betray a relationship that dates back 20 years. I first met her two decades ago in the aisle of a local lawnmower dealership. I can remember it like it was yesterday; she was sleek, attractive, trendy, and she purred like a kitten. Besides, my wife approved...

Before you get into this story much further, I want you know that I'm talking about my lawn tractor. I've had it 20 years this month, and I'm a little anxious about finally giving her up for something new. A man develops a special bond with his lawnmower over the years; at least I did.

I've resisted the temptation of test driving new models for years, but recently suspected that if there was lawnmower life-support, my old tractor would have been hooked up to a beeping monitor a few years ago. I could tell last fall that its innards were more willing than able to keep up with the demands I placed on it, so I began, albeit with a guilty conscience, to bring glossy sales brochures home, to ask friends about the particulars of their mowers, and to occasionally sit on display models (no, I didn't make put-put noises) in home improvement stores.

I'm somewhat of a lawn-mowing fanatic, but despite what my kids think, I have never used a tape measure to determine on what day I mow the lawn. I just enjoy seeing the grass neatly clipped; I feel my yard proves to people that I'm a reasonably neat person myself, that I take pride in what I own. I have no secret desire to be a greens keeper at a golf course, although I would love to mow the Red Sox logo onto the grass at Fenway Park someday. I've been known to mow my lawn in mid-summer when it's as crunchy and brown as a sugar cookie. I think the lines of a mowed yard give my life some organization, some symmetry, some semblance of control.

Over the years, my mower became a matter of pride for me. I often bragged that I managed to keep my tractor running while friends and neighbors bought new ones after theirs wore out. It has its original tires, has never needed an overhaul, and is only on its second set of blades. I believe that with proper maintenance, a man should be able to keep his machine going for years. I have been the model of mower upkeep: the master of mulch, the scraper of mower decks, the changer of oil, the guru of the grease gun. Yes, I even used to wax it every fall.

I come from a long line of frugal mowers. My uncle, a truck mechanic, rebuilt the engine of his old Cub Cadet a half-dozen times before he finally retired it to the scrap heap. My grandfather never had a riding mower at all; he bought his push mower at a dime store, and through diligent plug maintenance, filter replacement, and faithfully refusing to mow wet grass, he kept it roaring for years. My first mower as a home owner was second-hand; my father-in-law once broke it down in my garage and kept it rolling for me. Okay, we were all cheap.

A good buddy of mine has been after me for years to buy a zero-turn mower. He has one that can mow a yard the size of a small South American country in a few hours. It moves at warp speed and has an engine capable of powering a pickup truck; I think it came with attachments for char-broiling steaks and making ice, too. It was his mower that often came to mind while I sat in the broiling sun of an August day watching moles dig tunnels at speeds that exceeded my old tractor's top end. And, like a dolt, I have actually increased the size of my yard in recent years. "If mowing is so much work," my daughter says, "why do you keep making your yard bigger every year?"

But last fall, the handwriting was clearly on the wall; my mower's deck began to rust away, and I fought belts, and balky steering, and my seat (the tractor's) was just worn out. It wasn't a midlife crisis that drove me to seek another mower; I think the thing simply earned a little down time under a blue tarp in my barn, that's all. I finally broke down and bought a new model.

In 1987, Jim Baker publicly confessed his sins, Fred Astaire died, Oliver North took the Fifth, and the

DOW dropped over 500 points in a single day. It wasn't that great of a year, except that my son was born, and I bought my shiny new red mower with its spring-loaded seat, easy-lifting hood, and nifty hydrostatic drive. I still can't believe it's lasted so long.

Anyway, this summer, in between rounds on my new mower, I'm going to get my old tractor out, weld a little scrap over her see-through deck, apply a nice bit of duct tape to patch the seat, plump her tires, and mow bits and pieces of my yard for old time's sake. My son, who has become somewhat of a lawn-mowing obsessive-compulsive himself, will occasionally use it on his grandpa's yard. I hope I don't have to remind him to keep her oil and filters as clean as the day I brought her home. We may even slap a little paint on her bare spots and fix her headlights, because I truly believe that creaky old clipper still has a few yards left to mow.

True love does last forever.

Hummers prove that you can go home again
June 4, 2007

It appears to me that an abnormally cool April and an unusually warm May have left some of our plants and bugs and birds confused this spring. A few old-timers are telling me that it all points toward a very hot summer. I may have scientific faith in the National Weather Service, but I've also known enough back fence forecasters over the years to refuse to bet against their prognostications that we'll all be panting and praying for rain by the end of July.

One thing that I have noticed, along with the passing of a very poor mushrooming season, is that our hummingbirds seem to be slow to return to us this year. Despite looking for them to arrive on our doorstep by early May each year, a few pioneers almost always surprise us by taking an earlier flight, and they expect us to have our feeders full by late April. On occasion, the majority has spent a little extra time in Mexico before heading our way by mid-month, so my wife and I will stand by our picture window, a coffee mug or dish towel in hand, waiting to see one of the needle-nosed busybodies hovering near our woodpile for his fix of sugar water.

We have been anticipating more of them this week, since only two that we know of have made it home this year. Just this morning, my wife spied a female hummer near our kitchen window feeder. "I hope she's here for good and plans to have babies," she said, not unlike a grandmother who hopes that her brood of grandkids are coming back to the farm for a few weeks of country living and home cooking.

We are amazed by these aerodynamic specks of life. In a world where very few of us know in what direction we are headed, and so many of us are busy in our lives tearing things down and building things up, these birds find their way back to the same corner of Indiana to persistently await a free meal. I have read that they have traveled to us from exotic locales, from lands across the great Gulf, from the Yucatan, and their journeys take them through the spring thunderstorms and low pressure centers of the Midwest.

The rumor has it that hummingbirds hitch rides on the backs of larger birds as their frail bodies tire in their endless buzz to Indiana and points north. But I don't really believe that; they seem to be independent creatures, tireless and determined despite the fact that they travel all that way to take up rental cottages in my maple trees and gulp the nectar my wife boils on our stove all summer.

They do this as if some instinctual radar—some inbred global positioning system—hones in on turf that they know is their own. They must feel this as surely as any inner-city gang knows a favorite street corner.

In years past, we have counted as many as 30 or 40 hummingbirds hitting our feeders in a frenzy that's about as organized as a World War I dogfight over the trenches of France. Despite their delicate beauty, hummingbirds are fiercely territorial, often greedy. We have watched males cautiously guard their spots on feeders as tenaciously as their human counterparts hog television remotes. They spend much of their day like miniature hawks, leaving their posts only long enough to chatter warnings to thirsty intruders.

Through a fascinating National Geographic article I read a few months back, I learned that hummingbirds can beat their wings up to 80 times a second, and that their frail appearance is deceiving; they're tough little dudes. A perched hummingbird's heart rate is an impressive 500 beats a minute; there are 330 species of the them that live from "Alaska to Argentina," and their average body mass checks in at a mere five to six grams.

Writer Michael Klesius says that ruby-throated hummingbirds gather in Mexico in the very early spring, double their body weight by feasting on a smorgasbord of insects and nectar, then fly non-stop for 20 hours across the Gulf. I thought it was tough to load up the family car for a yearly vacation away from Indiana; look at what these wondrous bits of bone and feathers do to get here.

Several years ago, I watched a female hummer apparently lose control of her internal steering wheel and crash into my office window. I found her lying on the stifling concrete walkway, her breast heaving as her "cranberry-sized" heart furiously pounded. I was convinced she would soon die. She was no longer than my thumb and was already overdue for a hit of sugar water; hummingbirds eat virtually every minute of their day.

I asked my wife to deliver an eyedropper of her hummingbird elixir, and I pried the bird's forceps-like beak open and poured the water down her throat. In a few minutes, she was gulping it. In a few minutes more, she was perching on my forefinger, where she sat patiently between slurps from the dropper for another half-hour. Then, revived and revved, she flew to the bobbing branches of a nearby magnolia and was gone.

One day this September I will notice that the hummingbirds are suddenly gone. They'll be well on their luggage-less way back to southern warmth. But I feel I can be sure that they'll be coming home again in the spring. Perhaps we should be more like these flashes of green and red we admire from our kitchen window. They seem to know that they are temporary residents and look to get by one day at a time.

The difference between having nothing to do and doing nothing July 1, 2007

After my yard was mowed, my weeds pulled, and my tiny garden hoed today, I sat on our back step listening to the birds, staring off into the woods and soaking in the sun. It's not that I didn't have other chores to do; instead, I chose to do nothing. There's a difference between the two.

A month ago I watched a movie late into the night. It was about the life of Woody Guthrie, the folk-singer activist who rode the rails of the Great Depression from coast to coast, occasionally getting his head busted for trying to help unionize itinerant farmhands. In an early scene, Guthrie, who tried to eke out a living during the Dust Bowl days as a sign painter before doing much as a musician, was shown working on a grocer's sidewalk sale board. Around him, ragged, dirty, wide-eyed children watched as if his paint brushes were magic wands, spellbound by a man painstakingly working to make a dime.

I'm not going to preach a sermon here about how kids nowadays can't sit still without their video games or televisions supplying instant entertainment; I'm sure that if I were still a kid, I'd probably be as hooked on my cell phone and shopping at the mall as any young red-blooded American consumer is. But it seems to me that in our affluence, we have allowed our imaginations, our amazement at common, everyday wonders to atrophy. I think adults are as equally guilty of the same sin.

Doing nothing is indeed an art. Years ago, I read a poem by Walt Whitman called "Sparkles from the Wheel" and it became a favorite of mine. In it, Whitman describes how he stops along a boisterous city street to watch a man sharpen knives on a whirring stone. Along with a group of young children, he is captivated by the sparkles coming off of the stone as the "sharp-chinned" old man pressed the blade across it.

I remember doing much of that same kind of thing as a boy, myself. I was raised in a family that had pretty well banished the word "boredom" from its vocabulary. To tell my parents or grandparents that I was bored was an incredibly stupid thing to do; there was always yard work, or garden work, or house work to be done. So, as often as I could, I practiced the art of doing nothing, of tying knots in rope and wading the creek and getting my clothes filthy. Poet Robert Frost may have wished as an adult he could go back to his boyhood and once again be a "swinger of birches," but before I ever knew Frost's words, I had been a swinger of wild grapevines in my Cousin Renee's woods, performing stunts inspired by grainy black-and-white Tarzan movies from "The Early Show."

I wouldn't expect too many kids who are a fifth my age to run outside to try all I did as a reasonably fearless, often scabbed and bruised outdoors adventurer. I wouldn't suggest they fall out of their tree house, pole vault onto an old mattress with a sassafras limb, or wander a leech-filled branch. But I do have some suggestions for getting something out of doing nothing.

For instance, I'd like to see more kids read by flashlight under the covers at night when everyone else has gone to sleep. I'd like to see them build forts using kitchen chairs and old blankets. I'd like to know that they are lying in their back yards on cool nights watching the stars and wondering where people are going on those blinking lights they strain to see before they disappear into the blackness. I would hope that more kids fish for bluegill with their grandpas and bake cookies with their grandmas.

I know that youngsters have standardized tests and braces and practices of some kind or another to get to, but more of them should be able to fry bacon and eggs on a fire they built after a near-sleepless night listening to the sounds of the woods. I'd like to see them explore more sandbars in shallow creeks and learn how to skip rocks. They should feel the mud squeeze between their toes too.

Kids should still catch crawdads with strings; they should eat sun-warmed raspberries and blackberries just after they pick them themselves, even before they are washed. They should learn how to carefully open and close a pocket knife, and they should whittle. They should look for Indian beads, and they should hold a grasshopper in their hands.

Don't get me wrong; learning how to work is important too. But most of us learn how to do that early enough. Once we start earning a paycheck, doing nothing gets tougher, and it's obvious that if the government has anything to do with it, we will work until we are very old or die at our desks or factory production lines. So I think we need to keep doing nothing at least some of the time before we forget how.

I hope that while kids are still kids, they look at spider webs in the morning light, that they watch the sun both come up and go down in the same day, and that they get to keep a box turtle for part of a summer. I hope they get to fly a kite, watch waves crash onto a shore, and hum. I hope somebody teaches them how to whistle.

I'd like to know that some of them are watching little garden plots where they have planted seeds, that they are getting to eat peanut butter and jelly sandwiches, and they're still making ink out of the black juice of roadside walnuts. I want them to look very carefully at a bird's nest. I want them to play in the dirt, and I hope they have a place where they can simply sit in the quiet and listen. They should look at the moon through a telescope and pond water through a microscope at least one time.

Since I am done writing this story, I think I will go back to doing nothing. I'm still pretty good at it.

Going to war. . . in the backyard
May 5, 2008

My wife, God bless her, is always finding ways to make my family happy. She cooks our meals, does stacks of laundry, and keeps the house as neat as a pin. She tells me when my tie and shirt don't match, is willing to repeat dialogue I miss on the television, and tells me the yard looks good after I've mowed it; she often reminds me to take my prescription medicine, too. On most nights of the week, I'm in bed a good while before she's ever finished with the chores she wants to get done. I'm a lucky man.

But last week, I believe she took her love for me to a whole new level: She bought a set of plastic army men for me.

We had gone to an auction—a big one—and sitting on a shelf with glossy metal lunchboxes and classic comic books and other toys and memorabilia from my now distant childhood (the G.I. Joe footlocker brought back great memories), was a 32-piece "Action Army Set." Along the bottom of the original and dusty box, in particularly enticing red and black lettering, came the true siren song of advertising: "Have hours of fun with this exciting set;" and "Authentic detail!"

I must have been slobbering when I pulled the top off the box because she said, twice, I think, "We should get this; we may have a grandson who would like to play with it someday."

"Grandkid...I would play with it right now," I said, only half-kidding as I ogled the Patton tank and Army helicopter, the sounds of my own chopper-like special effects already reverberating in my head.

We had been keeping an eye on a few items at the other end of the building, so I took off to monitor the situation there, and when I returned, sure enough, she had bought the set. It went for $2; that was half of its original cost.

When I was a boy, plastic soldiers were my toy of choice. While other kids went for train sets or bows and arrows or metal backhoes and tractors, I wanted, above everything else, army men. I can't say exactly why. I wasn't raised in a particularly militant or bellicose family. Virtually all of my great uncles had been in World War II, but they hadn't come home with so many tales of battlefield glory that I was hooked on the idea of being in the military myself.

I think my love for the little green guys came from the movies. I had, after all, spent a good many Saturday and Sunday afternoons watching war pictures on Channel 4, films like "The Sands of Iwo Jima" and "Wake Island," and "Merrill's Marauders." My idea of real heroes came in the flickering black-and-white images of John Wayne and Brian Donlevy and Jeff Chandler, maybe even William Bendix, who almost always got himself killed.

My mom understood. I can still remember wandering the aisles of Woolworth's or Kresge's on Wabash Avenue whenever she took me downtown to shop, probably for pants since she could only patch my worn-out knees so many times. They were fascinating places, intimate little five-and-dimes, crammed floor to ceiling with everything from artificial flowers to thread to garden hoses, and, plastic soldiers—bags of them. Why you could buy a hundred for 89 cents, and more than once I recall meandering through the store searching for Mom, practicing my most pathetic, pleading expressions before I found her.

I had my own little army uniform too—a deep green outfit (actually, the trousers were old green jeans) that eventually grew too tight and too short in the arms. That and an authentic war surplus helmet—minus a badly-needed liner—made me a ridiculously scrawny soldier whose head disappeared in his too-big bean pot of a hat.

I stood at attention in more than one of my grandmother's photos in that uniform, and most often I was properly attired when I dragged my big box of soldiers out from under my bed for a rainy afternoon filled with the screams of grenade attacks, ambushes, and frontal assaults. More than once, Mom forced me to abandon my battlefield on the living room floor while she talked on the telephone, allowing me to continue with the whistle of mortar shells and the howls of banzai charges only after she'd hung up.

We lived in a wonderful place in those days. About fifty yards behind our house, under a massive red oak, was a big open sand pit. I spent hours there with those army men, planning massive battles, organizing tented encampments, building fortified pillboxes and machine gun nests with twigs and acorns and dirt clods. I imagine that if I were to go to that sacred place yet today, even after walking through it for the last time some 25 years ago, I might still uncover some lost and forlorn soldier, his arm forever primed and ready to hurl a grenade at enemy troops.

By the time my attention turned to basketball and girls and playing my brother's 45s on our portable record player, I had planned to annihilate my army men in one last Armageddon, but luckily, I never did. They collected dust under my bed for years until I left home and packed them away to await the arrival of my own kids.

When I was young, war was just a game. No one ever really died. My screams and moaning agonies were, thankfully, as phony as the movies I watched and the plastic men I played with. I know better now; the casualty lists that accompanied Walter Cronkite's voice on the evening news in the late 1960s sobered me some, and unfortunately have been replaced by no less tragic numbers from Iraq and Afghanistan.

But, in those days, I knew none of that, and the hours I spent with those soldiers, and on off days with my Fort Apache set or Civil War troops, was time using my imagination. It's too bad that all wars can't be fought that way.

A handful of reasons to take note of our hands
May 19, 2008

I've been working in my garden and yard these past few cool, wet weeks, and along with the progress I've made with the tilling and raking and mulching has been the satisfaction of seeing my hands toughen, not unlike an old catcher's mitt that's been neglected of oil and sweat and spit. Even a few calluses have been re-introduced to my palms, and I now have to scrub my nails with a brush in the evenings to drive the dirt out from under them. I think those are good things to see.

In the late fall, after I've put my rake and shovel and axe in the barn for the winter, my hands begin a gradual decline back to gentility and a life of indoor living. They don't take much of a beating in the winter, with the possible exception being extracted by hours with a cheap grading pen gripped in my right hand, perhaps the occasional run-in with sandpaper or firewood or snow shovel. My hands grow softer in the cold months, more pale, and my grip weakens without the proper exercise of clearing brush or shoveling rock or tossing the occasional bale of hay. Manipulating a keyboard does absolutely nothing at all for the cultivation of the personality of my hands.

I know that it's been said that our eyes are the windows to our souls, but I've always believed that it's our hands that lead the way in the development of our characters, of our grit and our get-up-and-go. I was raised to believe that a man, or woman, who would offer their hand to you in friendship, in a business transaction, perhaps even in reconciliation, was worth knowing and keeping as a friend. Even though it is my wife who has done the lion's share of child-rearing in my household, I believe I have taught both my son and daughter that a handshake is supposed to be firm, and that it shouldn't be offered unless it is honestly given.

Our hands tell others, perhaps more eloquently than our mouths, where we've been and what we've done with our years. Two friends, one gone now, one very much alive and strumming his guitar, lost fingers to table saws and tree-cutting fiascos years and years ago.

Herman Huxford, who passed some time ago, was an apostle of the merits of daily work, and I'd be willing to bet that he made a mile of oak baseboard and finished an acre of concrete, all for folks within a five-minute drive of his farm. Herman always said what was on his mind, but he was genuine and he was real.

Jim Trout, a veteran tree cutter who brought down a dying 100-foot sycamore near my house 25 years ago, has always reminded me of Herman Melville's Ahab, a chainsaw serving as his harpoon. Jim survived a lifetime amid the danger of falling timber, but he still laughs so easily that it solicits grins from everyone he meets. It's as if there became even more substance to him, and to Herman too, as their hands yielded precious area to the nemesis of sharpened steel.

Years ago I wrote a literary journal story about the

hands of my great-aunt, Grace. She outlived my grandmother by a couple of decades, but Grace's appearance, and her hands, were so strikingly similar to those of my grandma that to see her was almost painful, nearly frightening. Her hands, like Grandma Blanche's, were thick and soft and gentle. I think my cousin, Renee, inherited those hands; hers have the same look of those that I often saw as a boy when my grandmother sat at the quilting frames or stood at the canning stove or thumbed through her Bible.

My grandfather Roy's hands were remarkable too. They were larger than they should have been for a man who wasn't so big himself. He had the habit of always pointing at things, of standing at attention for photos with his hands open, his forefingers always askew. The hands that had gripped a pickaxe in coal mine shafts as a teenager and had dipped enameled pans by the thousands until he walked out of the factory for the last time to retire, could tie the most precise and delicate knots in fishing line I ever saw, and they could gently dig the roots of mature ginseng from the soil while leaving behind the tiny hair-like remnants of younger plants yet to grow. His hands could skin and scale and scour, but they could pat my head, plant corn in arrow-straight rows, and perfectly cast a fly rod.

A week ago, before I headed to my in-laws' for a Mother's Day celebration, I stopped at the cemetery. I was there to lay a few irises—my mom's favorite flower—on the gravesite she shares with Dad. It most often seems a solemn place, but on this trip I couldn't help but see their hands in my memories of them, and the work they did.

It was so easy to picture Mom's long slender fingers as they kneaded bread dough or darned a sock or turned the pages of a book. With Dad, I saw in my mind's eye the big freckles on his hands, and the scraped knuckles he consistently wore like badges of honorable labor, just like those described in poet Theodore Roethke's "My Papa's Waltz." Everything my folks owned, and much of what they gave to us three kids, came as a direct result of their toil and the time spent working with their hands.

Surely, there were slackers and thieves among my parents' and grandparents' generations; not all were heroic and stoic and uncomplaining. And there's little doubt that despite computer technology and an easier way of life brought to our doorsteps by hydraulic oil and diesel fuel, interstate highway, jet stream flight, and Ethernet cables, many among us still use our hands on a daily basis to turn the soil and hammer nails and to wash our pots and pans.

I'm glad for that. We need to take the time to do things the hard way every once in a while.